Silent Pastors
No Revival

· The Lies from Within ·

by Salvatore J. Varsalone, B.A. Religion

Library of Congress Control Number: 2011945365
ISBN: 978-1-890120-83-2

Design by: Mary Elizabeth Chupp

For additional copies, contact your local bookstore or:
    Greater Canton Youthquake
    3144 Forest View Street NE
    North Canton, Ohio 44721
    ph: 330 493 0749
    email: greatercantonyouthquake@yahoo.com

    Daystar Publishing
    Post Office Box 464
    Miamitown, Ohio 45041
    ph: 800 311 1823

Dedication

This book is dedicated to the over 800 kids who were led into the NIV by the Youthquake Ministry through Bible quizzing. The Ministry was deceived into leading you on the "wrong side of truth and history." Our sincere apology is needed.

Table of Contents

Acknowledgements vi

The Purpose of This Book. 1

The Author's Testimony on the Preserved Word of God 3

The Introduction (Understanding a little bit of history). 6

A Letter to the Pastor Who Just Didn't Know 35

Chapter One :: You and the Church Pastor. 37

Chapter Two :: You Just Found Out 43

Chapter Three :: God's View Concerning His Word. 49

Chapter Four :: A Comparative Study from a Spiritual View (See for Yourself). . . 59

Chapter Five :: Doctrinal Problems in the Counterfeits 67

Chapter Six :: More Doctrinal Problems in the NIV– Christ's Omnipresence 89

Chapter Seven :: More Evidence of Corruption (How much do you need?) 105

Chapter Eight :: Let's Talk About Revival 117

Chapter Nine :: So What Should We Do?. 129

A Letter to My Catholic Family and Friends 147

Beware! 153

Suggested Reading 155

Bibliography 157

Acknowledgements

First and foremost, with Jesus understood, I would like to express my gratitude to my beautiful wife Susie. Life without you could never be fulfilling. God gave me a wife who is loyal, faithful, and hard-working, and who loves me very much. Susie, you are also loved, and you are an example of the wife that is depicted in Proverbs 31. I am a very blessed man. I need not say anymore.

My family – you are always there for me.

In alphabetical order, I would like to recognize the following individuals whose many hours of hard work and prayers have helped to make this book possible. They are symbolic of the many Christians around the world who stand for the truth, but who receive little credit for all that they do for Jesus. None of you were looking for any credit, so allow me to brag on you a little bit.

The Belden Village Prayer Breakfast – Thank you to all of the men of the Belden Village Prayer Breakfast, who are led by Dr. Chet Bartram. This book was backed up with a lot of prayer. I was first alerted about counterfeit Bibles at this breakfast. It is one thing to pray, and it is another thing to pray for the truth. You do both. These men faithfully pray for a Repentance/Revival in the church every week.

Jim and Darcy Cicconetti – In October of 1973, while Jim and I served in the U.S. Air Force, stationed at Dover Air Force base in Delaware, Jim and Darcy Cicconetti led me to the Lord. They established me in a Bible believing church, where I began to study the Scriptures, and they encouraged me to serve the Lord in the church's bus ministry. Jim and I took Evangelism courses while at church as well. In my first year out of college, I met up with Jim and Darcy again, as I was invited to stay in their home for a few months, while I got established into the full-time ministry. Besides Jesus and my wife, no two people have had more of an impact on my life then Jim and Darcy Cicconetti. I am eternally grateful.

Ernie Cross – Thanks for all of your suggestions and for your advice. You helped with proofreading, and the cover of this book. You have been a good friend to me in several ways besides the tweaking of this book. You are so very knowledgeable on several subjects and very versatile. I am enjoying our growing friendship.

Weyandt Dettis – Thanks for the hours of proofreading that you did. All those notes were helpful. The questions that you asked helped me to rethink and confirm my position. You kept me on my toes. We have not known each other very long, but it has been a pleasure getting to know you. By the way, you are a great chess player.

Attorney Doug Fowler – Thank you for your service on the Youthquake Board of Directors. You always open up your home for the kids. You did so much proofreading and you did the dreaded bibliography. You are not only an inspiration to me, you are one of my best friends. I always enjoy talking baseball with you too.

Dr. Sam Gipp – You have been a friend and a mentor to me. I do not know what I would have done without your guidance on how to "publish" a book. Most of all, God really used you in helping me to understand the issue of the preserved Word of God in English. Your many books were most helpful because they all stand for the truth. You never ask anything in return from someone you have helped. You help them out of your love for Jesus. You helped me to be a better minister for our Saviour.

David Gnagy – No one can proofread faster than you. More importantly, the advice that you gave was invaluable, especially concerning "Marxism". Thanks for the book that you wrote called *Catamount*. The fictional story that you wrote was both entertaining and helpful in seeing the way things are in the age of Laodicea. It is a story within a story. You have a lot of knowledge Dave, and I believe your book should be a movie someday.

Pastor Joe Howland – You are always an encouragement, and you are always ready to pray. I can talk to you about anything. You have so much biblical knowledge with such sound doctrine. Thanks also for your proofreading and especially for the suggestion to do a little bit more history. You encouraged the whole "introduction" of the book.

Ernie Lautzenheiser – I know that I can always confide in you. You have a great listening ear. It is part of your ministry to people. God has used you to tell other people about counterfeit Bibles. Keep up the good work and thank you for all of your encouragement and for being a very good friend to me.

Ed Lytle – Thanks for serving on the Board of Directors of the Youthquake Ministry. While other board members were leaving the ministry, because of my stand on the preserved Word of God, you provided the leadership that was needed to steer the ship in the right direction. You brought Doug our way, and between the two of you, you allowed this ministry to preach the truth and not to compromise. I'm grateful for that and for your friendship and care for the

Youthquake Ministry.

Joe Samartino – You are an inspiration to me. I am so proud of the way that you have grown in the Lord since leaving Catholicism. Your desire for the truth, and the way you are learning your Bible at the Baptist church you attend, cheers my heart. Your advice on better writing style was very helpful to me, but your new relationship with Christ is the best.

Becky Sexton and the Former Catholics for Christ – Thanks Becky to you and all who wrote for the Former Catholics for Christ newsletter. All of you taught me so much when it came to the truth and where apostate Christianity is heading. There is a big difference in being involved in Christiandom and working with true brothers and sisters who are saved. Your discernment ministry was a big help to me as I had to sort out wrong teaching, which so easily makes its way into our doctrines. Thanks for all of your friendship and encouragement.

Charlie Tausch – I have a lot to say about you. When you read the manuscript of this book, you were compelled to leave your church, but only after your pastor did not give you the time of day. You tried to help him, and all he did was force you to leave by compromising your convictions. I am so glad that you found, and are now attending, a good Bible believing church, that preaches from the preserved Word of God. You are an example of the common Christian who will lead us to a repentance/revival because leadership chooses to remain so blind. God bless you.

Pastor Lonnie Trevino – Lonnie, your church had a team in my NIV Bible quiz league. During my investigation of counterfeit Bible versions, I came to you and asked you to look at the evidence of wrong doing on the part of these modern-day scholars. You spent much time reading the books that I put into your hands, and you concluded that the King James Bible was indeed the Word of God in English. You allowed me to present the evidence to your whole church. Together we convinced every member of your congregation, including the board of your church, to make the switch to the King James Bible. Thanks for standing with the preserved Word of God, and for being a responsible pastor, who treats his congregation with integrity.

the Purpose of this Book

The purpose of this book is to spark a repentance/ revival in the Christian churches in America and around the world. We are living in the age of Laodicea. Like the church *harshly* rebuked by our Lord (Rev. 3:14-22,) our churches have become:

Lukewarm... We do not have the enthusiasm to stand for the truth. We rarely evangelize the unsaved.

Rich and increased with goods... We preach a prosperity gospel.

With need of nothing... We depend on ourselves instead of God.

Wretched... We are very unhappy and with little joy.

Miserable... We do not have peace.

Poor... in our spirit, with little knowledge of the Bible.

Naked... Open to receive any wind of doctrine.

Blind... We could not see the truth if it were right in front of us.

There is no repentance/revival in sight. Yet we like to believe that we are doing well. We have mega churches in our city, yet there are people in our cities that remain unsaved. How has this happened?

The silence of pastors... Not what they are preaching,

but what they are *not* preaching.

The silence of denominational leaders… Make sure the pastor toes the line.

The silence of our college professors… Worship education.

The silence of modern scholars… *Change the Word of God.*

This silence has caused God to withhold His blessing from the churches. This silence is so loud, that the people cannot hear it. We will follow our pastors, even if they are no longer following God.

Therefore, we are very far away from any repentance/revival that will make an indelible mark on history. Unless we deal with the number one issue that is facing the church, and admit that there is a problem, we will never see a repentance/revival in our lifetime, and we will continue to move away from God and closer to the anti-Christ. The issue at hand concerns the preserved Word of God, which we have so blindly abandoned. Welcome, to Laodicea.

This book will seek to expose the many lies that live within the church. Information, deliberately hidden in most cases, must be given back to the "people." This book is meant to notify the average individual Christian, that most pastors, denominational leaders, professors in our colleges, and the modern Bible scholars, have changed the very Word of God for the worse. They refuse to tell the truth to the people, and they try to make those who oppose them, to look like they are the problem.

This book will examine how the counterfeit Bibles in our midst, have changed the doctrines of the church. Each major doctrine will be carefully examined and studied, so that the false teaching that is in the church today can be exposed. While the modern scholar likes to argue the history, and the Greek, and the manuscripts that are involved in the issue, this book would like to make a case for the spiritual evidence that is shown to all so very clearly, by doing a comparative study in the various Bibles that are involved, so that it will be clear for the seeker of truth, to discern in their spirit, the truth that the Holy Spirit wishes to impart.

This book is not meant to be a rehash of all the gory details that go into this argument, so as to bore the one who has knowledge of this issue, but instead, it is meant to alert the Christian who was robbed of this knowledge by the silence of their pastor. Hence, "Silent pastors will equal no repentance/revival because of the lies that go unchecked from within." It is time to open up our eyes, so that we may see. It is time to discern in our spirit, so that we may know and be sure. It is time to study to show thyself approved unto God, a workman that needeth not to be ashamed, rightly dividing the word of truth. II Tim. 2:15.

The Authors Testimony
On The Preserved Word Of God
(A short version of the whole story)

I put hundreds of kids in the NIV through Bible quizzing. I did not know any better. My college professors lied to me and told me that the NIV was the best Bible. My college professors told me that the NIV was easier to read, and easier to understand. I do not know if this misleading was intentional, or if this was an honest mistake. I will let God be the judge of the heart intention of men. Only He can know for sure. But I was still the one who was ultimately responsible to check this out for myself. However, at that stage in my life, the Holy Spirit was not leading me to make any change in the Bible that I was using. I never knew that there was a controversy over the different Bibles being used by the churches. I was preoccupied with just being a student.

I believe that my professors knew how to hold back certain information that they did not want me to study. For instance, they did not want me to know that the Greek text I was using was that of Westcott and Hort. (These men were two Anglicans who never professed Christ as their personal Saviour. These men were trained by the Roman Catholic Jesuits.)

I have come to realize how biased they were concerning the stand that they were making for the modern Bibles. I was told that the Bible I had in my hand was the closest to the Greek. I did not know that there were several different Greek texts. I always thought that when they were talking about the Greek, they were referring to the originals. I found out later in my life that the originals were lost.

The denomination, to which I belonged, was experiencing a serious debate, within its leadership, concerning whether to abandon the *"preserved Word of God in English,"* the King James Bible. This debate went on behind *closed doors.* The flock was *not* invited to this debate, and neither were the students.

I did not understand this at the time, but I remember that there were some people who left the denomination because they did not like the changes that were made in the Bible that the denomination decided to use. There was no vote that was taken among the people. The leaders of the denomination made this decision between themselves. I discovered later, that the denomination's leadership was heavily influenced by one of their scholars who worked on the committee of Bible translators of the NIV.

In 1996 the Lord used four housewives, who wrote for the newsletter of the former Catholics for Christ, and a friend of mine from a prayer breakfast, to show me that I must get the kids in my ministry out of the NIV. We were Bible quizzing on the local, regional, and national level. Our teams were doing very well. I was very concerned, and this is when I began to do an intense investigative study. I was overwhelmed with all of the conflicting information. It was time to consult the Lord and ask some questions and to pray for wisdom.

This was the first time in my life that I realized the different versions of the Bible were distinctly different. I began to compare and I could not believe how different the Bibles were that I was comparing. I discovered that there was a "preserved text of the Bible," and that my college had used the "corrupted text of the Bible." One had its manuscripts in Antioch Syria, and the other had its manuscripts in Alexandria Egypt. God destroyed the originals because He wanted us to walk by "faith" and not by "sight."

I began to see that the versions of the Bible like the NIV, NASB, RSV, and the MESSAGE, etc. were from Alexandria Egypt. Nothing good in the Bible is ever said of Egypt. Such counterfeits are *displeasing to God.* I had the kids in my ministry on the *"wrong side of truth and history."*

In my ministries Bible Quiz League, after I made the switch from the NIV to the authorized King James Bible, I lost board members, friends and more than one third of my "missionary support." The devil tried to drive my wife and I out of the ministry. The Lord, however, saw fit to replace my board with a board that allows me to teach the *truth.* I made new friends, and the Lord replaced most of the income that I lost. I now contend for the faith in this "vital area of ministry."

I am deeply concerned for the "flock," and for a "repentance/revival" to break out in the Christian churches both in America and around the world. Attorney Doug Fowler, a member of my board said, *"We must also pray without ceasing.* This is a spiritual battle. We must clearly see that there is a problem that must be addressed. We must stand for the truth concerning God's preserved Word and seek God's guidance, provision and protection."

The Lord showed me from a "spiritual point of view," that the post 1881 versions of the Bible in English are COUNTERFEIT. As I surrendered to the Lord on this issue, He also proved to me in an intellectual and historical way as I studied church history on this subject, that I could contend for the faith and truly show others, in an accurate way, what their pastors, in most cases DO NOT WANT THEM TO KNOW.

Before we look at a comparative study, where you could see for yourself what has been hidden from you, let's take a look at some very basic facts concerning the *history of the Bible*. In the "introduction" we will look at the *"preserved line of manuscripts"* in history, and the *"corrupt line of manuscripts"* in history. This will not be an extensive history because the best work that I know on the subject, is listed in the suggested reading section. *Gipp's Understandable History of the Bible* is a detailed work that I will use as a basic reference point. Besides the Bible itself, I highly recommend this book to all who want to know the history of the Bible. Another great book, that is very handy to have, explaining the history that is involved in this issue, is *A Charted History of the Bible,* by James C. Kahler. You will see very clearly what the devil tried to do to render the Word of God useless, since he cannot destroy it.

The Introduction

(Understanding a little bit of history.)

God loves us so much that He desires to have an *intimate* relationship with the human race that *He Himself* created. He communicates to all mankind in the following ways:

1. God speaks to us by His Holy Spirit through our *mind*.
2. God speaks to us by His Holy Spirit through our *heart*.
3. God speaks to us by His Holy Spirit through other *people*.
4. God speaks to us by His Holy Spirit through *circumstance*.
5. God speaks to us through *nature*.

But most of all God speaks to us through the person of Jesus Christ, who is God in the flesh, and through His written word.

The Bible *itself* talks to us about the *feelings* of God concerning the Bible that He gave to us. There are many verses in the Bible *about* the Bible. Preservation verses are mentioned throughout this book, as well as the many other books that have been written on this subject. Psalm 12:6-7 is one of the strongest verses in the Bible that attests to the preservation of God's Word.

"The words of the Lord are pure words: as silver tried in a furnace of earth, purified seven times. Thou shalt keep them, O Lord, thou shalt preserve them from this generation forever."

If God wants man to have His Word, throughout all the ages of history, He Himself will have to preserve it. God loves the Bible that He inspired so much that the Bible itself tells us that it is the most important thing to Him.

Psalm 138:2 states, *"I will worship toward thy holy temple, and praise thy name for thy loving kindness and for thy truth: for thou hast magnified thy word above all thy name."*

If God had to choose between His *very name* and the *Word* that He wrote to us, He would pick His *Word*. His Word means everything to Him. God just has to *speak* the Word and it is *done*. Surely you can see why God, *who never changes,* does not want man to change His Word. Let's take a short trip through history, and see the differences in the two timelines and how the English Bible was produced. One timeline is *preserved*. The other timeline is *corrupt*. You will clearly see what side of history is represented by God's ability to *"preserve"* His Word, and what side the devil has used to *"corrupt"* His Word.

The "Preserved" Line

God

God *desired* to speak… so God *inspired* a Book… then God *preserved* the Book… then God *authorized* the Book… and now it is sufficient even up to the last universal language of the world which is English. Over the course of some 1,500 years, God used around 40 different authors to produce His Word in *seven* different *universal* languages of the world.

The Old Testament

The Old Testament was written by *Holy Men of God* as they were moved by the Holy Spirit. This was done by the will of *God* and not by the will of *man*. The apostle Peter records it this way in 2 Peter 1:21:

"For the prophecy came not in old time by the will of man: but holy men of God spake as they were moved by the Holy Ghost."

This is called *"inspiration."* A verse to look up on this can be found in II Timothy 3:16.

"All Scripture is given by inspiration of God, and is profitable for doctrine, for reproof, for correction, for instruction in righteousness."

The Old Testament was written in Hebrew. Hebrew was the *first* universal language of the World. The *Levite* priests were in charge of preserving the Scriptures. The *scribes* painstakingly wrote on the scrolls that housed the Scriptures. If they made one mistake, they wrote the Scripture on the scrolls *all over again.* The Old Testament was also written in Aramaic. Aramaic is the *second* universal language of the world. Just a few books were written in Aramaic. Part of the book of Daniel was written in Aramaic. The preserved Hebrew Old Testament is called the *"Masoretic text."* The Old Testament was completed around 400 B.C. The first five books were written by Moses. There are 39 books of the Old Testament. The Jews did a great job in preserving the Old Testament.

The New Testament

The New Testament was written in Koine Greek. Greek was the *third* universal language of the world. The New Testament is made up of 27 books.

The writers were:

Matthew	Paul
Mark	James
Luke	Peter
John	Jude

Paul wrote 12 of the books of the New Testament for sure, and most historians believe that he was the author of the book of Hebrews as well. That's almost half. The other writers combined, wrote the other half of the New Testament. John wrote 5 of the remaining 14 books. The last book of the New Testament was written by John about 95 A.D. on the island of Patmos. John died on Patmos about the year 98 A.D. The early church had their writings and preserved their works. The manuscripts came from Antioch Syria where Christians were first called Christians.

The Old Testament was read in the churches as well as the Gospel writings, and the letters. God placed no specific value on the *"originals."* Dr. Sam Gipp says in his book, *Is our English Bible Inspired?,* "If God left the *originals* intact, we would have an *idol.*"[1]

To explain several of the following sections, I will lean heavily on direct quotes from the book, *A Charted History of the Bible* by James C. Kayler.

The Autographs

"The New Testament autographs were written after the resurrection of Christ. All 27 books, written largely in Greek, had been finished around A.D. 95 when John completed Revelation. As far as we know, all of the autographs have been either lost or destroyed because of their aged and decayed condition.

The New Testament books were most likely written on papyrus, an early form of paper. Instead of using clay tablets or parchment, men like Matthew, Mark, Luke, and John wrote on the smooth surface of the papyrus. Although it was easy to write on, it became very brittle and fragile with age. Thus, no autographs of the New Testament have survived."[2]

---

1. Gipp, Samuel. *Is Our English Bible Inspired?* (Daystar Publishing: Miamitown, 2004) p. 15.
2. Kahler, James. *A Charted History of the Bible.* (Daystar Publishing: Miamitown, 2007) p. 15.

The Traditional Text

"The *Traditional Text* refers to the accurate and reliable manuscripts that come from Antioch, Syria as well as manuscripts that agree with the Antiochan manuscripts. After Jerusalem was destroyed in A.D. 70, Antioch became the center for Christian evangelism. With a vital emphasis on a historical, literal, interpretation of Scripture, Antioch also naturally became a center for the preservation of the Bible. Scripture was copied, distributed, and most importantly, viewed literally as God's perfect Word. By the end of the first century, over 100,000 Christians were living in Antioch.

"Antioch was the primary location for Bible preservation, but it wasn't the only location. The 'traditional text' was preserved at Pella in Palestine, by the Italic Church in Northern Italy, by the Gallic Church in southern France, by the Celtic Church in Great Britain, by the pre-Waldensians, by the Waldensians, and by the churches of the Reformation.

"Other names for the Traditional Text include: Antiochan Text, Byzantine Text, Imperial Text, Majority Text, Reformation Text, Syrian Text, and Universal Text. Over 5,500 manuscripts and the broad evidence of history support the Traditional Text."[3]

The Syrian Peshitto

God did not choose to keep the Bible in Greek only. The early Greek manuscripts were translated into many other languages in order that the true Word of God could be put into the hands of people in other lands. Dr. Gipp states in *Gipp's Understandable History of the Bible,* that "The Peshitto was translated from the Greek about the year 150 A.D."[4] There were other well-known versions of the Bible such as the Gothic, Sahidic, Bohairic, and the Coptic. Syrian was the *fourth* universal language of the world. Dr. Gipp also states that "The Peshitto is actually *older* than our oldest uncial manuscripts."[5]

---

3. Ibid.
4. Gipp, Samuel. *Gipp's Understandable History of the Bible.* (Daystar Publishing: Miamitown, 2000) p. 59
5. Ibid.

The Old Latin Vulgate

The Old Latin Vulgate is dated about 157 A.D. This translation is not to be confused with the Latin Vulgate of Jerome in 395 A.D. Latin became the *fifth* universal language of the world and remained the universal language of the world throughout the *"dark ages."* Many Christians in the *"dark ages,"* other than the Catholics, had the *"preserved Word of God"* available to them. Christian sects like the *Paulinists, Monatist, Donatist, Waldensians,* and the *Albigensis* were persecuted by the Catholic Church that dominated church history from around 400-1400 A.D. The "dark ages" lasted about 1,000 years.

The Roman Catholic Church did not believe in putting the Scriptures into the hands of their people. Even though Jerome took the word *"vulgate"* which means *"common,"* the Catholic people were left in the dark when it came to the Scriptures. Bible believing Christians had to read their Bible without the Roman Catholic authorities knowing about it. You could be executed for having a Bible in your home. Many Christians in history died a martyr's death by the killing hand of the Roman Catholic Church. Research the "Spanish Inquisition." You should also research the book, *Fox's Book of Martyrs.* (See suggested reading section.)

John Wycliffe

I am going to list John Wycliffe as being on both the *"preserved line"* and the *"corrupt line."* I will try to explain.

John Wycliffe was the first man to translate the Scriptures into English. He got the ball rolling about the year 1380. The "textus receptus" of Erasmus was not yet available to him. Wycliffe's intentions seemed noble, but he ultimately drew from the corrupted manuscripts that the Roman Catholic Church made available to him. He really belongs on the *"corrupt line"* but not because he himself had any wrong intentions. There is no evidence that I know of that indicates any wrong intention on the part of John Wycliffe. So we will give him this mention and later explore him further, but on the *"corrupt line"* and not the *"preserved line."*

I will continue with some more direct quotes from the book, *A Charted History of the Bible* by James C. Kahler, to cover the following sections that explain the *"preserved line."*

Erasmus Greek New Testament

"Desiderius Erasmus (1466-1536) compiled Traditional Text manuscripts and produced a Greek New Testament in 1516. His goal was that everyone would be able to read the Bible, from the farmer in the field to the weaver at the loom. After his death, Erasmus' text was revised by men like Robert Stephanus (4 editions) and Theodore Beza (10 editions). It was Beza's fifth edition (1598) that was to be the basis for our English King James Bible." Dr. Samuel C. Gipp, *Gipp's Understandable History of the Bible,* Third edition, 113

"The Elzivir brothers edited Erasmus' New Testament and published three editions. Written in the preface of the 1633 edition was the following statement: "You have, therefore, the text now received by all, in which we give nothing changed or corrupt." From then on, all editions of this text became known as the *Received Text,* or the *Textus Receptus.*

"Erasmus' work was monumental in that it made the Greek text available in Europe. The *Textus Receptus* helped to ignite a spiritual explosion known as the Protestant Reformation and in less than 100 years had been translated into over 16 languages. It served as the basis for the New Testaments of a number of reliable English Bibles, the best being the King James Version."[6]

Tyndale's Bible

"William Tyndale (1494-1536) translated the New Testament from the *Textus Receptus* in 1525. The Tyndale Bible (which was only the New Testament) became the first English Bible to be printed on a press. Because England was still under Roman Catholic rule, Bible translation was illegal. Therefore, Tyndale moved to Germany to print his Bibles and smuggled them back into England in sacks of corn and flour and bales of hay (some 3,000). Later, Tyndale returned to England, and in 1535 was arrested, and later strangled and burned at the stake

---

6. Kahler, p. 15.

(1536). His final words were, 'Lord, open the eyes of the King of England.'

"In honor of his good textual work, William Tyndale is called the 'Father of the English Bible.' Much of his translation is reflected in the King James Version. Between 1535 and 1568, a total of six English Bibles were published, each based on the *Textus Receptus* or another Bible which was based on the *Textus Receptus*.

Coverdales' Bible (1535)

"Miles Coverdale (1488-1569) was the first to print a complete English Bible (Old Testament and New Testament). He relied on Tyndale for the New Testament."

Matthew's Bible (1537)

"When Tyndale was arrested in 1535, he managed to pass the manuscripts of his unpublished Old Testament to his friend John Rogers (1500 – 1555). Rogers published a new Bible using the pseudonym Thomas Matthew, hence *Matthew's Bible*. Sixty-five percent of Rogers' Bible comes from Tyndale with the remaining 35% borrowed from Coverdale. In 1535 during the reign of 'Bloody Mary,' Rogers was placed under house arrest and later burned at the stake. Witnessing his death, were his wife and eleven children."

Taverner's Bible (1539)

"The Taverner's Bible was a business venture by publisher Thomas Bertlelet. Because he needed a Bible that wasn't exactly like Roger's, he used a manuscript produced by Richard Taverner. Taverner's work was mostly a revision of the Matthew's Bible.

The Great Bible (1539)

"The Coverdale Bible and the Matthew's Bible, both endorsed

by King Henry VIII, circulated England, each with a different terminology and phrasing. Bishops in England felt the people needed ONE Bible. Instead of making the difficult choice between the Coverdale Bible and the Matthew's Bible, a new translation was approved. Miles Coverdale became the editor and used the Matthew's Bible as the basis for the new version instead of his own."

The Geneva Bible (1557)

"Under the reign of 'Bloody Mary,' a number of godly and learned men fled from England to Geneva, Switzerland. Among this number of refugees were William Whittingham, Miles Coverdale, and John Knox, who began at once to work on a new translation, which would become known as the Geneva Bible. The New Testament portion of the Geneva Bible was based on Tyndale's Bible."

The Bishop's Bible (1568)

"In many ways, the Bishop's Bible was nothing more than a revision of the Great Bible, which was a revision of the Matthew's Bible, which was 65% Tyndale. Translated by several bishops of the Church of England, the Bishop's Bible was intended to replace the Geneva Bible. Although every cathedral and bishop was ordered to have a copy of the Bishop's Bible, the Geneva Bible remained the favorite for home and personal use. Much of England would use the Geneva Bible until the middle of the 1600's when another Bible—the historic King James Version—would replace it in popular affection."[7]

Martin Luther's German Translation of 1522

Just three years before Tyndale's Bible was published in England, Martin Luther published a Bible in German. It should be mentioned on the "preserved line." English was fast developing as the last universal language of the world. German was number *six* for a short time. The reformation had just started

---

7. Kahler, p. 16.

in 1517 and by 1522 Luther had translated the Bible into German. Dr. Gipp states again in *Gipp's Understandable History of the Bible,* that the "Tide of the reformation soon came sweeping across all of Europe until it washed the very shores of England." The already weakened authority of Rome was devastated by the *onslaught of truth.*[8]

The King James Bible of 1611

What a Bible it was and *is* today. The *seventh* and final universal language of the world *was,* and *still is* today, *English.* English started slowly as the universal language of the world around 1400. The Bible experienced 7 purifications in fulfillment of Psalm 12:6-7, which when that Psalm was written, *was prophetic.*

The King James Bible is the Bible that the Roman Catholic Church loves to hate and tried to destroy. The Roman Catholic Jesuits, who were formed around 1546 during their church's *"counter reformation,"* came up with a plot to kill King James I of England.

This plot is recorded in history as the *"gun powder plot."* The parliament was about to take place...an anonymous warning was issued...five assassins who were all Roman Catholic Jesuits were found in the basement with gunpowder. It was a failed attempt to assassinate King James I of England. This happened on October 26th 1605. You can look up this date for a check on the facts on the internet.

The *"gun powder plot"* was Satan's second attempt in history to stop the King James Bible from being written. The first attempt came on May 29, 1588, when Pope Sixtus V combined with King Philip of Spain attempted to overthrow England. They should have done it because Spain had a navy that was superior to England's navy. A great armada sailed for England. *However,* God intervened because while the Spanish Armada was sailing across the English Channel, a storm perked up and wiped them all out. Spain lost 79 ships and about 17,000 men.

A *third* attempt of Satan was to try to get an *eighth* English Bible onto the scene in 1610. He knew what was coming. The Roman Catholic Church produced the Douay Rheims Bible in 1610. It was translated from Jerome's corrupt Latin Vulgate of 395 A.D. These manuscripts were from the *"corrupt"* line of Scripture, taken from *Alexandria Egypt* where nothing in the Bible was ever

---

8. Gipp. *Gipp's Understandable History of the Bible,* p. 45.

said in a positive way. Remember Satan's MO…If you can't beat them, then, join them. We will look at the *"corrupt"* line of manuscripts out of Egypt after we finish this *"preserved line."* We will briefly trace the major steps that show how our English Bible became *corrupt*.

Everything about the production of the King James Bible was *honorable and positive*. God enabled King James I of England to assemble the greatest scholars of the day. King James recognized that England needed a translation that would *unify* the country behind a single English Bible. The Great Bible was too cumbersome. The Geneva Bible was too controversial. The Bishop's Bible was too careless.

On July 22, 1604, King James placed his official authorization on the proposal. On that same date, King James announced that he had selected 54 men to translate the Bible into English. They must all be proven scholars and that they were. The meticulous work began in 1607. England was destined to become the greatest most powerful *nation* in the world. Its conquest would carry them to every continent. Everywhere they went, an English Bible would accompany them. When God and the Bible are connected to history you see things more spiritually. It took 7 years to complete. There is that number 7 again!

Surely, three significant events in history happened in the age of Philadelphia. This is the age described in the Bible before the age of Laodicea. The description of Philadelphia is all *positive*. God said that because *"Thou hast kept my Word."* I will give thee *"An open door."* Read Revelation 3:7-13 to see how God describes the age of Philadelphia, which is the age of time before the age of Laodicea. Here are those 3 significant events in history that happened in this age:

1. 1517 – The Protestant Reformation. Starting with Luther's German Bible, the people now had the Scriptures in their *hand*. The Roman Catholic Church was weakening. Mystery Babylon (the Roman Catholic Church) was being exposed for creating its doctrines outside of the Word of God. The Reformation broke the dominance of the Roman Catholic Church. Freedom in Christ took hold and many great preachers brought revival to the land that made an *"indelible mark on history."* The Roman Catholic Church has never been the same. The only thing that stayed the same in the Catholic Church was that it refused to change the false doctrines that it created outside of Scripture.

2. 1611 – This was the year that the King James Bible was completed. England was the most powerful country on earth in 1611. King James gathered the

greatest Bible scholars of all history to unite all of Christianity on one Bible. But the Catholic hierarchy, and not the common people, were using their corrupted Douay Rheims. The Bible believers were using the purified precursor Bibles, and then God authorized the final production of the Bible in English, the King James Bible. Yes, a *"translation"* can be inspired. Dr. Gipps book *Is Our English Bible Inspired?* is listed in the suggested reading section of this book. This book will explain how God went about "inspiring and preserving" the Scriptures.

3. 1776 - The establishment of the United States of America. The only country in world history that used the *Bible* in its constitution was the United States. The United States of America quickly grew into the most powerful country in the world! By 1776 most Christians had flocked to the King James Bible.

The people flocked to the English Bible naturally on their own because it was such a great translation which was done in the purest of English, the *"Elizabethan dialect."* Most of the Puritans used the Geneva Bible because they did not like King James. The Geneva Bible also drew from the preserved line of manuscripts, but the Puritans could have chosen the best work that was ever done which was the *"authorized King James Bible."* But they didn't. Remember, all authority is given to us by God. Nonetheless, the people finally had a Bible *in their hand.*

The scholars that King James I of England chose to translate the Bible into English, were the greatest Bible scholars the world has ever seen. They were honorable men with integrity. In I Samuel 2:30 it says:

"Be it far from me; for them that honour me I will honour, and they that despise me shall be lightly esteemed."

They never brought any attention to themselves. Compared to the scholars of today, they were head over heels *"superior scholars"* who drew from the Majority text known as the *"textus receptus."* This means the *"received text."* The manuscripts were from Antioch Syria in the preserved line after the 7 predicted purifications of the Bible. Just to name a few, here are some of the names of these scholars and their qualifications:

John Reynolds

He began college at age 13.

At age 23 he obtained a position as a Greek lecturer.

He had a solid reputation as a Greek and Hebrew scholar.

He later became president of his university.

He was known for his incredible memory.

He memorized entire manuscripts and books.

He could easily find the page, column and paragraph of a particular text.

Reynolds made the official request to King James that an accurate translation of the Scriptures be made.

Lancelot Andrews

He was the Dean of Westminster and the Chaplain to Queen Elizabeth.

His nickname was: *Star of preachers.*

He was fluent in 15 languages.

He would often take a one month vacation to study a new language under a master.

He did his daily written devotions in Greek.

Such was his skill in languages that it was said, "That had he been present at the confusion of the tongues at Babel, he might have served as an interpreter."

John Bois

He could read Hebrew at age 5.

He could write Hebrew at age 6.

He attended St. John's College where he gained a mastery of *another* language, Greek.

He later became a Greek lecturer at the college.

He owned one of the most impressive personal libraries of Greek literature.

He spent up to 16 hours per day in study.

He was a member of the 12 person committee who made the final review of the translation.

Conclusion

Shortly after the King James Bible was completed, the people *flocked to it*. All the English speaking people, except for the Puritans, used the King James Bible. Just about all of *"biblical Christianity"* was *united* on *one* Bible for about 270 years. The greatest revivals in history were possible because of the King James Bible. Could you imagine the Bible studies that they had, and how they went without any of the *confusion* we see today?

God's final work in English was done in the *"purist"* of the English language.

No one ever talks about changing Shakespeare in any way. It is a *classic.* So is our English Bible. Our English Bible does the following:

It… Rhymes.

It… Sings.

It is… Poetic.

It has… Alliteration.

It is… Easy to memorize.

It is… A 5th grade reading level.

James C. Kahler sums up the King James Bible like this:

"The King James Version built upon the strengths of the earlier English Bibles. It rivaled its predecessors in simplicity and literary excellence, but the greatest improvement was the text itself. The translators had a better grasp and understanding of the original languages (Hebrew and Greek), enabling them to produce a Bible that was a faithful and more accurate translation of the very words inspired by the Holy Ghost.

When the Bible was translated in 1611, God foresaw the wide extended use of the English language; and therefore, in our Authorized Bible, gave the best translation that ever has been made, not only in the English language, but as many scholars say, ever made in any language." Dr. David Otis Fuller, *Which Bible*, Fifth Edition, pg. 316.

The "Corrupted" Line

The *"preserved line"* began with God. The *"corrupt line"* must begin with Satan. Nothing burns up Satan more than the *"word of God."* Nothing is more dangerous to the truth than a *half lie*. Satan is a great liar. He is the *father of lies*. Corruption of the Scriptures began in Genesis chapter three. We must go back to Genesis to see how Satan first began to corrupt the word of God. You can sometimes catch a *full lie*, but a *half lie* is tough, because it is mixed with some *truth*. Moses records the conversation between Satan and Eve in Genesis 3:1-5:

Satan

"Now the serpent was more subtle than any beast of the field which the Lord God had made. And he said unto the woman, Yea, hath God said, ye shall not eat of every tree of the garden?

Satan was saying to Eve… God told you that you could not eat from all the trees in the garden?

"And the woman said unto the serpent, we may eat of the fruit of the trees of the garden:"

We can eat the fruit in the garden.

But of the fruit of the tree which is in the midst of the garden, God hath said, Ye shall not eat of it, neither shall ye touch it, lest ye die.

But the tree in the middle, (which was the tree of knowledge) we cannot eat from that one or we will die, even if we touch it!

And the serpent said unto the woman, Ye shall not surely die:

So the devil calls God a liar. He is telling a half truth because Adam and Eve did not drop dead when they sinned. The death that God was talking about was a spiritual death which would result in a physical death later. Hence, the need for all Christians to be "Born Again," lest they die twice.

For God doth know that in the day ye eat thereof, then your eyes shall be opened, and ye shall be as gods, knowing good and evil.

God is hiding something from you Eve. You can eat from that tree. The only reason God doesn't want you to eat from that certain tree is that you will know good and evil like He does. As a matter of fact, you will be as a god too! Don't believe God!

You know the rest of the story. Satan lied to Eve, who deceived Adam, and man fell out of fellowship with God. Satan changed the words that God said, to make it appear that God did not know what He was doing. Satan attacked the very words of God, and declared war on God, and charged God with being a liar. The Word of God is still being attacked by Satan today, especially in the English language. Satan hates the Word of God more than anything.

Satan hated, and attacked God's Word from the garden, up to the time of Christ. Satan never stopped his opposition against God when the church was formed. He got even angrier, and more hateful. Since we are concerned about the "English Bible," let's look at the history of the "corrupted line" where the eventual corrupted versions in English got their start. We will begin with Justin Martyr.

Justin Martyr

Justin Martyr (103-165) was an early Christian apologist who was interested in philosophy. Much of what we know about him came from his own writings. He was born in Flavia Neapolis (today Nablus) in Palestine. *His parents were pagan.* He tried the school of a stoic philosopher, who was unable to explain God to him. He then attended a Peripatetic philosopher, who was more interested in collecting his fee. He then moved on to a Pythagorean philosopher, who demanded that he first learn music, astronomy and geometry, which he did not want to do. After this he was drawn to Platonism. He had a great pagan history.

He met an old man, whom he did not name, on the seashore, who told him about Christianity, and he converted. He then adopted the dress of a philosopher himself and traveled about teaching. He arrived in Rome in the reign of Antoninus Pius (138-161), where he started his own school. This school was the beginning point of what was to be known as the "school of Alexandria," which was eventually developed by "Clement of Alexandria."

Paganism was being mixed with Christianity. Justin Martyr was really known as Justin, son of Priscus. He became known as Justin Martyr because he died a martyrs' death. It is fair to say he had some *unbiblical doctrines.* He did not believe that Jesus was God. He believed that Jesus was a *"created being"* created by the Father. He did not understand the biblical Godhead. Does this sound familiar? I know that you have heard of the Jehovah Witnesses!

Justin Martyr began to adjust the Scriptures to his own liking, as he combined the philosophies of his background, and pretty much started his own theology. I guess he had a "dynamic equivalent" of the Word of God. Later on, after his martyrdom, the Roman Catholic Church and the Greek Orthodox Church would canonize him as a saint. You can go on the internet and study about Justin Martyr in more detail. Much of the Bible's corruption came out of the school that he had started. The devil was going to keep this ball rolling. Justin Martyr had many students that studied under him. One of his students was a man named *Tatian*.

Tatian
(110 – 180)

Tatian was a student of Justin Martyr. Simply put, Tatian was a Gnostic. Gnosticism was a heresy that grew into the early church. It taught that Salvation comes from secret knowledge granted to initiates. I do not have any idea what that means. The sources of Gnostic beliefs range from Babylonian, Egyptian, and Greek Mythology. Gnosticism threatened the doctrines of the Early Church. It declined somewhat after the second century, but lives today in most of our modern English versions of the Bible, and in the doctrines that they corrupted.

Tatian leaves out genealogies of Matthew and Luke and passages that spoke of Jesus as David's seed from the work he produced called his *"Diatessaron."* His Gnostic views led him to exclude from the continuous narrative of our Lord's life, given in this work, all those passages which bear upon the Incarnation and the Deity of Christ. Tatian was a forerunner to the "school of Alexandria" which was started by Clement of Alexandria.

Clement of Alexandria
(C. 150 – C. 215)

Titus Flavius Clemens, or Clement of Alexandria, was a student of the stoic philosopher Pantaenus. Clement drew extensively on Philo, and followed both Philo and Justin Martyr. He relied heavily on Greek Pagan Philosophy, and tried to unite this philosophy with Christianity. Clement spent much time defining for the Christians the originally pagan philosophical concept of the "logos." He had a very *"transcendent"* god.

Clements' mixture of Stoicism and Platonism brought about heresies in several doctrines like the Deity of Christ and the Incarnation. Clement maintained that the body of Christ was not subject to human needs.

Clements' parents were wealthy pagans from Athens. Alexandria was his bishopric. His best known pupil was Origen. He succeeded Pantaenus as the head of the *"catechetical school of Alexandria,"* or the *"school of Alexandria."*

With Clements' help, corruption of the preserved Christian manuscripts came into existence, so that paganism could better fit with Christianity. Clement believed that all sin has its root in ignorance, and that the knowledge of God and of goodness is followed by *"well doing."* In essence, he preached *Salvation by Works.*

Origen
(185 – 253)

Origenes Adamantius, otherwise known as Origen, was born of Christian parents in Egypt. He was a theologian who spent most of his life in Alexandria as a teacher. He succeeded Clement as the head of the "catechetical school" in Alexandria. He too, adulterated the Gospel with pagan philosophy. The chief accusations against Origen's teaching are making the Son inferior to the Father and thus being a precursor of Arianism, a fourth century heresy that denied that the Father and Son were of one substance.

Origen spiritualized away the resurrection of the body and he denied that there was a hell. He believed in *Universalism.* He dissolved redemptive history into a timeless myth by using allegorical interpretation of the Scriptures. He turned Christianity into a Gnosticism which said that the spirit is good, but that *all* matter is evil.

The main contribution of Origen concerning the corruption of the Scriptures lies in his work called the "hexapla." The Hexapla is the six corrupted Greek text of the Bible written by Origen. He is probably the real producer of the Septuagint which was written about 250 A.D. Most of the modern-day scholars want to date the Septuagint around 250 B.C. but according to Dr. Peter Ruckman, all the evidence points to Origen. Dr. Ruckman goes into this history in detail in his book, *Manuscript Evidence.* This book is in the suggested reading section. Origen's "ecletic rescension" of the Septuagint had significant influence on the codex Sinaiticus which was used by Jerome. Jerome translated the Catholic Bible into Latin in 395 A.D.

The Minority Text
(Sinaiticus and Vaticanus)

As Kahler notes,

> "The Minority text Sinaiticus and Vaticanus represent only 5% of all existing manuscripts. The school from Alexandria Egypt produced the text sometime in the middle of the fourth century. The Minority texts were rejected by the "early church" and the 'protestant reformers' for the following reasons:
>
> "The Minority texts were the work of unbelieving Egyptian scribes who did not accept the Bible as the Word of God or Jesus as the Son of God!
>
> The Minority texts abound with alterations, often a single manuscript being amended by several different scribes over a period of many years; something the Aaronic priests and the Masorites would never have tolerated when making copies of the Scriptures."[9]

The Minority texts omit approximately 200 verses from the Scriptures. This is equivalent to I and II Peter. The Minority texts contradict themselves in hundreds of places. The Minority texts are doctrinally weak and often dangerously incorrect.

Every English version of the Bible relies on the Minority texts except the King James Bible. The King James Bible relies on the Textus Receptus.

Jerome
(C. 347 – C. 420)

The Roman Catholic Church was on the scene in Church History with the donation of Constantine around 315 A.D. Many historians claim that the donation of Constantine, in reality, was a Roman Catholic *forgery*. Nonetheless, Constantine made Christianity the *"religion of the Roman empire."* The Bible preaches a separation of church and state. Matthew 22:21 says to:

"Render therefore unto Caesar the things which are Caesar's; and unto God the things that are God's."

The Roman Catholic Church does not believe in separation of church and state. God does not force Himself on anyone. You choose to believe by your own *"free*

---

9. Kahler, p. 19.

will." Church History would be dominated by the Roman Catholic Church from 400 – 1400. History records the time as the *"dark ages."* I wonder why?

Popery was in full swing. It had its origins in the pagan Roman Empire even before Christ came on the scene. Pope Damasus I appointed Jerome as his confidential secretary and librarian. Damasus commissioned him to work on translating the Bible into Latin. They called the work of Jerome the *"Latin Vulgate."* He borrowed the term *"Vulgate,"* from the *"old Latin Bible,"* which means *"common."* The Catholic Bible was only *"common"* to the Catholic Hierarchy. The Hierarchy did not put the Bible into the hands of the people. Even the priests were left in the dark concerning the Bible unless they taught theology.

Instead of drawing from the manuscripts available to him, solely, from the "old Latin Vulgate" of 150 A.D., Jerome drew from the corrupted manuscripts of Alexandria Egypt, and from the school that was started by Justin Martyr. Paganism was being mixed with Christianity. Paganism was now influencing the translation of the Bible into Latin. True doctrines of the Christian Church were getting changed. Books have been written about the paganism associated with the Catholic Church. I will list a couple of them in the suggested reading section.

In his interpretation of the Bible, Jerome used both the allegorical method of the Alexandrian text, and the realism of the Antiochan text. But the compromise of the Scriptures was now supported by the Roman Catholic Church. Jerome's Latin Vulgate would be the Bible used by the Roman Catholic Church for the next 1500 years. Jerome mainly used the Minority texts in translating the Bible into Latin, for the unbiblical Roman Catholic Church. The heart of biblical corruption now had the support of "mystery Babylon."

John Wycliffe

It was mentioned that the intentions of John Wycliffe were noble. He was placed on the "preserved line" because he was the first person to translate the Bible into English in about 1380. He really belongs on the "corrupt line" because of the following reasoning captured again by James C. Kahler:

> "John Wycliffe initiated a translation that would become the
> first complete English Bible. Wycliffe, who lived from around
> 1328 to 1384, was a philosopher, theologian, church reformer,
> and, as Archbishop Thomas Arundel stated, a "perfect liver."

His desire was for the flock of his day to have a Bible they could read.

"In Wycliffe's day, Bible reading, even among the clergy, was surprisingly rare. As one of his disciples put it, it was thought sufficient if the priest knew the Ten Commandments, the Paternoster (Our Father), the Creed and Ave (Hail Mary), 'with common parts of holy writ.' The ordinary Christian knew even less. Benson Bobrick, *Wide as the Waters*, 49.

"Wycliffe did not know the original languages of the Bible, but he did know Latin, and therefore translated his Bible from Jerome's Latin Vulgate. Because the Wycliffe Bible is based on Jerome's Latin Vulgate, it is not a reliable Bible. In spite of the unreliable nature of the Wycliffe Bible, John Wycliffe wet the appetite of the English-speaking people for a Bible in their native tongue. In this regard, Wycliffe played a very pivotal role in later English translations of the Bible.

"Wycliffe died in 1384, and consequently was not able to complete the Bible that bears his name. Two versions of the Wycliffe Bible exist: the first done under the supervision of Nicholas. Nicholas was one of Wycliffe's disciples, and the second completed under John Purvey, Wycliffe's secretary.

For translating the Bible into English, the Roman Catholic Church, through the Council of Constance (1414), condemned Wycliffe as a heretic and ordered his bones to be exhumed. In 1428, under a decree from Pope Martin V, Wycliffe's remains were burned and his ashes scattered in the Swift River."[10]

The Douay-Rheims Version of the Bible

By the middle of the sixteenth century, there were many Protestant Bibles in several languages, especially English. The Protestant Church of England was a Bible reading church. English-speaking Catholics, on the other hand, had no approved English Bible of their own. James C. Kahler explains it this way:

"Theological issues so captured the imagination of people in the sixteenth century that they discussed such questions as part of daily conversation.

10. Ibid, p. 20

Protestants could argue from their Bibles and quote their notes. Catholics had nothing to help them. So for the sake of the Catholic minority and in the hope of somehow bringing England back to the Catholic Church, church leaders decided the time had come for an approved Catholic English translation with proper notes. John Stevens Kerr, *Ancient Texts Alive Today: The Story of the English Bible*, 100.[11]

Enter
The Roman Catholic Jesuits
and
Westcott and Hort

The age of "Philadelphia" preceded the age for which we now live. We live in the most *"rebuked"* age in history. We live in the age of *"Laodicea."* The devil knows that his time is short. The devil knows that he has lost the war. He hates God, and God's Word, more than anything else in the world. He knew he must attack the Word of God in English if he was to be successful in getting more people to follow him.

Enter the Roman Catholic Jesuits and Westcott and Hort. The Roman Catholic Jesuits trained Westcott and Hort. Westcott and Hort wrote the *"corrupted Greek text"* that underlies most of the modern Bible versions. This *new* "corrupted Greek" text began to be written in 1881. Can we trust the Roman Catholic Jesuits? You be the judge. Have you ever read the "oath" that the Roman Catholic Jesuits must take? I will reproduce this in its entirety from the author Gary H. Kah who wrote the book, *The New World Religion* starting on page 316:

> Appendix K:
>
> SPECIAL NOTE... Before you read this, I want you to compare the Spirit and message of Jesus, who told Peter to put away his sword, and the Holy Spirit living inside of you as a saved Christian; to *Nazi Germany,* the *Mafia,* and the oath taken by the *Freemasons.* Here it is:
>
> *The Ceremony of Induction and Extreme Oath of the Jesuits*
> "When a Jesuit of the minor rank is to be elevated to command, he is conducted into the Chapel of the Convent

---

11. Kahler, p. 20.

of the Order, where there are only three others present, the principal or superior standing in front of the altar. On either side stands a monk, one of whom holds a banner of yellow and white, which are the Papal colors, and the other a black banner with a dagger and red cross above a skull and crossbones, with the word INRI, and below them the words IUSTUM, NECAR, REGES, IMPIOS. The meaning of which is:

"It is just to exterminate or annihilate impious or heretical kings, governments, or rulers.

"Upon the floor is a red cross upon which the postulant or candidate kneels. The Superior hands him a small black crucifix, which he takes in his left hand and presses to his heart, and the Superior at the same time presents to him a dagger, which he grasps by the blade and holds the point against his heart, the Superior still holding it by the hilt, and thus addresses the postulant.

The Superior

"My son, heretofore you have been taught to act the dissembler: among Roman Catholics to be a Roman Catholic, and to be a *spy* even among your own brethren; to believe no man, to trust no man. Among the Reformers, to be a Reformer; among the Huguenots, to be a Huguenot; among the Calvinists, to be a Calvinist; among the Protestants, generally to be a Protestant; and obtaining their confidence to seek even to preach from their pulpits, and to denounce with all the vehemence in your nature our Holy Religion and the Pope; and even to descend so low as to become a Jew among the Jews, that you might be enabled to gather together all information for the benefit of your Order as a faithful soldier of the Pope.

You have been taught to insidiously plant the seeds of *jealousy* and *hatred* between communities, provinces and states that were at peace, and incite them to deeds of blood, involving them in war with each other, and to create revolutions and civil wars in countries that were independent and prosperous, cultivating the arts, and the sciences, and enjoying the blessings of peace. To take sides with the combatants and to act secretly in concert with your brother Jesuit, who might be engaged on the other side, but openly opposed to that with which you might be connected; only that the church might be the gainer in the end, in the conditions fixed in the treaties for peace and that the *end justifies the means.*

You have been taught your duty as a spy, to gather all statistics, facts and information in your power from every source; to ingratiate yourself into the confidence of the family circle of Protestants and heretics of every class and character, as well as that of the merchant, the banker, the lawyer, among the schools and universities, in parliaments and legislatures, and the judiciaries and councils of state, and to "be all things to all men," for the Pope's sake, whose servants we are unto death.

You have received all your instructions heretofore as a novice, a neophyte, and have served as a coadjutor, confessor and priest, but you have not yet been invested with all that is necessary to command in the Army of Loyola in the service of the Pope. You must serve the proper time as the instrument and executioner as directed by your superiors; *for none can command here who has not consecrated his labors with the blood of the heretic; for "without the shedding of blood, no man can be saved."* Therefore, to fit yourself for your work and make your one salvation sure, you will, in addition to your former oath of obedience to your Order and allegiance to the Pope, repeat after me."

The Extreme Oath of the Jesuits

"I, M_____ N_____ now, in the presence of Almighty God, the blessed Virgin Mary, the blessed Michael the Archangel, the blessed St. John the Baptist, the holy Apostles St. Peter and St. Paul, and all the saints and sacred hosts of heaven, and to you, my ghostly father, the Superior General of the Society of Jesus, founded by St. Ignatius Loyola, in the Pontificate of Paul the Third, and continued to the present, do by the womb of the Virgin, the matrix of God, and rod of Jesus Christ, declare and swear, that his holiness the Pope is Christ's Vicegerent and is the true and only Head of the Catholic or Universal Church throughout the earth; and that by virtue of the keys of binding and loosing, given to Holiness by my Saviour, Jesus Christ, he hath power to depose heretical kings, princes, states, commonwealths and governments, all being illegal without his sacred confirmation and that they may safely be destroyed. Therefore, to the utmost of my power, I shall and will defend this doctrine and His Holiness' right and custom against all usurpers of the heretical or Protestant authority whatever, especially the Lutheran Church of Germany, Holland, Denmark, Sweden and Norway, and the now pretended authority and churches of England and Scotland, and branches of the same now established in Ireland and on the Continent of America and elsewhere; and all adherents in regard that they be usurped and heretical, opposing the sacred Mother Church of Rome. I do now renounce and disown any allegiance as due to any heretical king, prince or state named Protestants or Liberals or obedience to any of their laws, magistrates or officers.

"I do further declare that the doctrines of the churches of England and Scotland, of the Calvinists, Huguenots and others of the name Protestants or Liberals to be damnable, and they themselves damned and to be damned who will not forsake the same.

"I do further declare, that I will help, assist and advise all or any of his Holiness' agents in any place wherever I shall be, in Switzerland, Germany, Holland, Denmark, Sweden, Norway, England, Ireland, or America, or in any other kingdom or territory I shall come to, and do my uttermost to extirpate the heretical Protestants or Liberals' doctrines and to destroy all their pretended powers, regal or otherwise.

"I do further promise and declare, that notwithstanding I am dispensed with, to assume any religion heretical, for the propagating of the Mother Church's interest, to keep secret and private all her agents; counsels from time to time, as they may entrust me, and not to divulge, directly or indirectly, by word, writing or circumstance whatever; but to execute all that shall be proposed, given in charge or discovered unto me, by you, my ghostly father, or any of this sacred convent.

"I do further promise and declare, that I will have *no opinion or will of my own,* or any mental reservation whatever, even as a corpse or cadaver (*perinde ac cadaver*), but will unhesitatingly obey each and every command that I may receive from my superiors in the Militia of the Pope and of Jesus Christ.

"That I will go to any part of the world whithersoever I may be sent, to the frozen regions of the North, the burning sands of the desert of Africa, or the jungles of India, to the centers of civilization of Europe, or to the wild haunts of the barbarous savages of America, without murmuring or repining, and will be submissive in all things whatsoever communicated to me.

"I furthermore promise and declare that I will, when opportunity presents, make and wage relentless war, *secretly* or *openly*, against all heretics, Protestants and Liberals, as I am directed to do, to extirpate and exterminate them from the face of the whole earth; and that I will spare neither age, sex or condition; and that I will *hang, burn, waste, boil, flay, strangle and bury alive* these infamous heretics, rip up the stomachs and wombs of their women and crush their infants' heads against the walls, in order to annihilate forever their execrable race. That when the same cannot be done openly, I will secretly use the *poisoned cup,* the *strangulating cord,* the *steel of the poniard* or the *leaden bullet,* regardless of the honor, rank, dignity, or authority of the person or persons, whatever may be their condition in life, either public or private, as I at any time may be directed so to do by any agent of the Pope or Superior of the Brotherhood of the Holy Faith, of the Society of Jesus.

"In confirmation of which, I hereby dedicate my life, my soul and all my corporeal powers, and with this dagger which I now receive, I will subscribe my name *written* in my *own blood,* in testimony thereof; and should I prove false or weaken in my determination, may my brethren and fellow soldiers of the Militia of the Pope cut off my hands and my feet, and throat from ear to ear, my belly opened and sulphur burned therein, with all the punishment that can be inflicted upon me on earth and my soul be tortured by demons in an eternal hell forever!

"All if which I, M_____ N_____, do swear by the blessed Trinity and blessed Sacrament, which I am now to receive, to perform and on my part to keep inviolably; and do call all the heavenly and glorious host of heaven to witness these my real intentions to keep this my oath.

"In testimony hereof I take this most holy and blessed Sacrament of the Eucharist, and witness the same further, with my name written with the point of this dagger dipped in my own blood and sealed in the face of this holy convent.

(He receives the wafer from the Superior and writes his name with the point of his dagger dipped in his own blood taken from over the heart.)

Superior

"You will now rise to your feet and I will instruct you in the Catechism necessary to make yourself known to any member of the Society of Jesus belonging to this rank.

"In the first place, you, as a Brother Jesuit, will with another mutually make the ordinary sign of the cross as any ordinary Roman Catholic would; then one crosses his wrists, the palms of his hands open, the other in answer crosses his feet, one above the other; the first points with forefinger of the right hand to the center of the palm of the left, the other with the forefinger of the left hand points to the center of the palm of the right; the first then with right hand makes a circle around his head, touching it; the other then with the forefinger of his left hand touches the left side of his body just below his heart; the first then with his right hand draws it across the throat of the other, and latter then with his right hand makes the motion of cutting with a dagger down the stomach and abdomen of the first. The first then say *iustrum*; the other answers *Necar*; the first then says *Reges*. The other answers *Impios*. (The meaning of which has already been explained.) The first will then present a small piece of paper folded in a peculiar manner, four times, which the other will cut longitudinally and on opening the JESU will be found written upon the head and arms of a cross three times. You will then give and receive with him the following questions and answers."

Ques. From whither do you come?

Ans. From the bends of the Jordan, from Calvary, from the Holy Sepulchre, and lastly from Rome.

Ques. What do you keep and for what do you fight?

Ans. The Holy faith.

Ques. Whom do you serve?

Ans. The Holy Father at Rome, the Pope, and the Roman Catholic Church Universal throughout the world.

Ques. Who commands you?

Ans. The successor of St Ignatius Loyola, the founder of the Society of Jesus or the Soldiers of Jesus Christ.

Ques. Who received you?

Ans. A venerable man in white hair.

Ques. How?

Ans. With a naked dagger, I kneeling upon the cross beneath the banners of the Pope and of our sacred Order.

Ques. Did you take an oath?

Ans. I did, to destroy heretics and their governments and rulers, and to spare neither age, sex, nor condition. To be as a corpse without any opinion or will of my own, but to implicitly obey my superiors in all things without hesitation or murmuring.

Ques. Will you do that?

Ans. I will.

Ques. How do you travel?

Ans. In the bark of Peter the fisherman.

Ques. Whither do you travel?

Ans. To the four quarters of the globe.

Ques. For what purpose?

Ans. To obey the orders of my General and Superiors and execute the will of the Pope and faithfully fulfill the conditions of my oath.

Ques. Go ye, then, into all the world and take possession of all lands in the name of the Pope. He who will not accept him as the Vicar of Jesus and Vicegerent on earth, let him be accursed and exterminated.

"*Special Note Continued…* So what did you conclude? Wasn't that wonderful? No wonder Judas killed himself when he found out that Jesus was not going to usher in a "political kingdom!"[12]

Another Note

This Jesuit oath is located in the Library of Congress, Washington, D.C., and Library of Congress Catalog Card # 66-43354. A nearly identical version of this oath may be found in the U.S. House Congressional Record, 1913, P. 3216. The oath was originally made public in the year 1883.

Westcott and Hort

Westcott and Hort wrote the Greek text that underlies most of the modern Bible versions in English after 1881. They were influenced by the Roman Catholic Jesuits. Neither man really gave testimony that they were saved by grace through faith. They believed the theology of the Roman Catholic Church. Dr. Gipp puts it this way in Gipp's *Understandable History of the Bible,* pages 37, 232-233.

"By 1870 England was ripe for Westcott's and Hort's radical ideas. Higher education had been casting doubt on the King James Bible for years. Their Greek Text, based on a handful of poor quality Egyptian manuscripts rather than the *irrefutable majority* was used by the Revision Committee of 1871 in an effort to supplant the King James Bible. It, or a variation of it, has been the text used by almost every revision and version ever

---

12. Kah, Gary P. *The New World Religion.* (Hope International Publishing: Carol Stream, IL 1999), p. 316.

since. This text of theirs, which is entirely Egyptian in origin, relies on nothing more than a handful of inferior Egyptian manuscripts which had already been rejected centuries earlier by the church as a whole. They had languished, unused and neglected until these two apostate scholars took up their cause and foisted them on Christianity.

"So the battle began! Which text is closest to the "originals"? Which manuscripts are "most reliable"? And, of course, the ultimate question: "Do we have a perfect Bible in English today?"

"Dazzled by Westcott and Hort's slight of hand, Bible colleges and learned men all over England jumped on the Egyptian bandwagon and faithfully promoted the Westcott & Hort theory while heaping scorn on the God honored text of the King James Bible. As a result of this, many young ministerial students had their faith in God's ability to preserve His Words assailed, and then finally had their perfect Bible replaced with an inferior English copy of the African text. As young pastors, these deceived young men occupied pulpits across the country and around the world and immediately began to parrot their professors, seeking to dislodge the King James Bible from the hearts, minds and hands of believers.

"Today, as we enter the Twenty-first Century, Christianity is still divided over the question, 'Do we have a perfect Bible in English today?' This battle will probably continue in this century as it did in the 20th, if the Lord tarries His coming."[13]

The Confraternity Bible

The American Bishops' Committee of the Confraternity felt the need to replace the Douay-Rheims Bible with something more readable. The Biblical Commission at Rome approved the project and work began on the new version in 1936. This Catholic Bible was based on an edition of the Latin Vulgate. The New Testament was published in 1941. This Bible is not on the preserved line.

---

13. Gipp. *Gipp's Understandable History of the Bible*. pp. 37, 232-233.

These Bibles are not on the preserved line:

The Revised Standard Version, The New America Standard Bible, The NIV, The Message, The Living Bible, The New World Translation, The Amplified Bible, The Jerusalem Bible, The New International Inclusive Language, The English Standard Version

Special note on the New King James - The New King James also draws from the corrupt text. It appears to be not as bad as the others, but it is more dangerous, because it makes people feel that it is a King James Bible. That is far from the truth. The New King James is the "King Agrippa of Bible versions." Using the New King James Bible is like almost being saved. There is nothing new under the sun. Ecclesiastes 1:9.

"The thing that hath been, it is that which shall be; and that which is done is that which shall be done: and there is no new thing under the sun."

Only ten versions of the corrupt Bibles from Alexandria Egypt are listed. There are about 200 other versions of the Bible in English from these corrupt texts. Not one of them says the same thing in different places of the Bible. Hence, there is much confusion. This concludes the "corrupt line." Which Bible do you have in your hand?

A Letter To The Pastor Who Just Didn't Know

Dear Pastor,

I would like to thank you for your dedicated service to Jesus Christ. I believe that the highest vocation in life is serving in the pastorate. Pastors have an enormous responsibility and there are many pressures that are placed upon you that the flock does not understand. I realize that our Christian pastors are not perfect people, and those pastors who are honest about their imperfection will freely admit this. Since no one is perfect, you are allowed, as I am, to make an honest mistake. I want you to know that *this book is not meant to be an attack on you.*

Rather than an attack meant to hurt you or your ministry, this book is meant to help you and your church to *reach its fullest potential in all that God has planned for you,* and for your church to experience many people getting *saved* at your *altars*, due to your dedicated preaching from the *"preserved Word of God."*

Unlike God, who in Himself is unchangeable, we humans must change all the time. It shows our level of growth. God always exalts those who are humble. The Bible tells us that *pride* comes before a *fall*. Do you remember when you preached on that subject?

So it is with the sincerest intention, that this book is written to the flock, so that *they* may know how to discern whether the Bible that you are preaching from, and that *they* are reading, is the preserved Word of God in English, and not a counterfeit Bible that you have mistakenly lead them to believe is all right with *God*.

Your response to this book might help to spark a repentance/revival that is so crucially needed in the church today. There is no shame on those who are able to admit that they have made a mistake. The *blinded* will refuse to see the *truth* presented in this book. The flock will make sure that they know the difference between a pastor who just didn't know, and a pastor who is *indifferent*. The *blinded* will also refuse to see how vital this mistake is going to cost the church from experiencing a *renewal*. Besides the Bible itself, there are many great books, so much better than mine that I have recommended for you to read that will assist you out of this *mess*. I have sought the forgiveness of God in the mistakes that I have made in my ministry, and I pray that you will do the same.

I can *testify*, that after God purged me and led me through the fire, I came out *forgiven and strong*, and most of all, I came out *free*. He will do the same for you. It is my prayer that you will accept *responsibility* for leading your congregation on counterfeit Bibles, and seek God's guidance concerning the crucial decisions you must now make. *Let revival begin with you.* Who else in the church is there to lead us? God bless you as you ponder your decision. May your church be richly blessed, and may God open up the eyes of those who did not see this coming. The Youthquake Ministry will do all that it can to help you if you want it to. We will come to your church and help you adjust.

Sal Varsalone,
The Youthquake Ministry

Chapter One

You and the Church Pastor

Our pastors will be the key figures in a repentance/ revival if one were to break out. But, I am not confident that they want to lead us through this issue. Most of our pastors ignore this situation unless they find themselves challenged by the people who know what they are talking about. *They seek to keep the people uninformed.* It will be up to you, as an individual, to bring this issue to the forefront. If a great work for Jesus is to get done, it will take the common person to take the lead in revealing the corruption that has our pastors preaching from counterfeit Bibles. Look into what you can do to *help* your pastor. The idea is to solve the problem and not to participate in adding fuel to the fire by causing problems in the church. But unfortunately, the problem is already here, so let's examine how this problem relates to you and the pastor of your church:

"And he gave some, apostles; and some, prophets; and some, evangelists; and some, pastors and teachers." (Eph. 4:11.)

The pastor is part of the New Testament's *"fivefold ministry."* (Notice that priests are not listed.) Surely, there is a very special place and position for *pastors* in the New Testament Church. Our pastors are to be *respected* and *remembered*. In Hebrews 13:7 the Lord says:

"Remember them which have the rule over you, who have spoken unto you the word of God: whose faith follow, considering the end of their conversation."

In verse 17 God says:

"Obey them that have the rule over you, and submit yourselves: for they watch for your souls, as they that must give account, that they may do it with joy, and not with grief: for that is unprofitable for you."

We read further instruction in I Thessalonians 5:12-13:

"And we beseech you, brethren, to know them which labour among you, and are over you in the Lord, and admonish you; and to esteem them very highly in love for their work's sake. And be at peace among yourselves."

Finally, in I Tim. 5:17 the Bible says:

"Let the elders that rule well be counted worthy of double honour, especially they who labour in the word and doctrine."

The Bible is very clear. God has placed spiritual leaders over churches, and these leaders are *rulers* who are to be *honored, obeyed,* and *loved* by Christians. God is the one who called the *pastor* of your church into service for Him. So, by all means, if your pastor is like the verses above, he deserves your *loyalty*, your *support*, and your *prayers*. We should do this in *obedience* to God.[14]

But this does not mean that your pastor is always right. Neither does it mean that your *pastor* is always *walking with God.* There are pastors today who are not speaking to you *"the Word of God."* They are not *"watching for your soul."* They are not *"ruling well."* Many are just collecting a *paycheck.* You never see them outside the walls of their church. As long as there is *money* in the church they are *comfortable.* Few pastors actually live by faith as our missionaries live. *They get a set salary.* This does not apply to all, but there are many pastors who *fit the bill.*

Even among many who have been called by God, there are *pastors* who are not, *"labouring in the word and doctrine."* Although there are many pastors who are truly *"walking with God,"* most pastors, in the Age of Laodicea, do not follow *"all the counsel of God."* (Acts 20:27.)

Most pastors in the Age of Laodicea are *preaching from counterfeit versions of the Bible.* And most of them *"do not care."* We are the ones who are letting them

---

14. Taken from a tract produced by Central Baptist Church, Canton, Ohio

get away with it. We do not ask them *questions* for fear of disturbing the peace. From where will the accountability of the pastor come, if they do not preach from the *"preserved Word of God?"* Should it not come from the very people that they hurt? God is already holding them accountable. We are reaping the curse of the *Laodicean mentality.* Hopefully, we are not as blind as the pastors who are leading us into these counterfeit Bibles.

What, then, should the average Christian do if his/her *pastor* is not *preaching from the Word of God*? Should he/she *leave the church*? What if your pastor is *open* to *being taught*? Is there a difference between a *pastor* who is *ignorant*, and a *pastor* who is *indifferent*? If your *pastor* is not preaching from the *"preserved Word of God"* should we not, *first*, go to him? The Bible tells us that if we have a problem with our brother, we should, *first*, go to our brother before we take a witness with us. After we have brought a witness, we should take the issue before the *church*. At this point, if the issue goes unresolved, then we are to give this person up to being a heathen and a publican. (This principle is found in Matt. 18:15-17.)

So by all means… FIRST, go to *your pastor.* God put this principle in the Bible for good reason. We should always follow the biblical procedure when there is a problem in the church. Going to your pastor alone is the first thing you should do.

Could there be an explanation as to why your *pastor* allowed himself to be *deceived by others*? I know for myself, I was ignorant. I failed to study to show myself approved of God concerning Bible versions. I depended too much on my college professors. I trusted them without knowing what was really happening. Our *pastors* are important to a repentance/revival. The blessings of God in our churches are at stake. The *ball* must be *passed to you,* the average Christian, if we are to be successful in allowing God to bring about a *revival.* What do you want to do about it?

You have a responsibility to consult with your *pastor* on this issue. But you will need to do some homework. We sometimes look up to our pastor as if he were GOD. Don't get me wrong. I am not talking about being disrespectful. I am talking about your God-given right to *spiritually discern.* If we think our pastors are perfect, we are committing *idolatry* by placing someone on the same level as God. Only God is perfect. People make mistakes. Your *pastor* could be wrong in the *vital issue of the "preserved Word of God in English."* Even when it is concerning your *pastor*, you must *rightly divide the Word of Truth.* You can also know the truth by following the Holy Spirit and by knowing your Bible. Your pastor does not necessarily have a special insight on the truth that you cannot *also* discern.

The Scripture says in I John 2:27:

"But the anointing which ye have received of him abideth in you, and ye need not that any man teach you: but as the same anointing teacheth you of all things, and is truth, and is no lie, and even as it hath taught you, ye shall abide in him."

There are pastors who are "called" but do not know why they were led to believe they should *abandon* the *"preserved Word of God."* Some pastors do not even believe the Bible is *"inerrant"* and *"preserved."* They will show themselves with their *indifference on the subject of God's preserved Word.* I have found that most *pastors* have never done a *serious* comparative study concerning the issue of counterfeit Bibles. Yet, they remain *blinded and unreachable.* When in the pulpit, you will often hear your pastor say, "The Word of God says," but if you heard him in a debate on the issue, he, more than not, will proclaim that the Word of God is not perfectly preserved. He will defend *"textual criticism"* and his *"alma mater."* But he will sell out the "preserved Word of God in English." Textual criticism destroys our faith and confidence in God preserving His Word. Textual criticism corrects God.

So, what will you do if your pastor fits into this category? Are you equipped and prepared? These are tough questions, but it has come down to *the people taking charge,* because the *denominational leaders* and the *scholars* in the universities have a tight hold on most *pastors.* Therefore, they have *a tight hold on you.* Our pastors are not taking the lead in bringing up this issue and educating you on the facts. Rather, they *ignore* it. Don't let them get away with ignoring you. Ask the hard questions and let your pastor discern the truth with you by letting the Holy Spirit lead. *The comparative Scriptures will speak for themselves.*

Most people are in the dark concerning the origin of the Bible that they are reading, and hold dear. *Which of the more than 200 Bible versions in English is God's?* There are over 200 different English versions of the Bible, and they are not saying the same thing. Not only are they not *saying the same thing,* they are no longer saying the *"right thing."* We are no longer saying the *"right thing"* concerning important Christian doctrines. We have left ourselves to be openly scrutinized by any false religion because we Christians are not united in our own Bible. *How can we do this to ourselves?*

The one area we should be *united* is in the very Bible that we claim as our *final authority.* It is the King James defender who seeks to be united in the one and only Bible in English that God gave to us. God does not need 200 different versions of His Word that are not saying the same thing. Remember, the anti-Christ will promote a *false peace* and a *false unity.* However, it will not be the anti-Christ who will promote a unity when it comes to the Bible. The King James scholars have been accused of adding to the Scriptures. *This accusation is false.* Textual critics must justify their subtraction of the Scriptures, so they accuse those who stand for *inerrancy*, and who have the highest of *integrity*, of adding to the Scriptures. Can you see the devil adding anything to the Word of God to make it better? The devil doesn't add much of anything. He adds nothing to *faith, hope or love.* The devil just subtracts from all of these things, including the Bible.

The Post 1881 versions of the Bible have *contradictions and severe errors concerning major Christian doctrines. We will examine every major Christian doctrine, in a comparative study, in chapters five and six of this book.* In Chapter four you will be able to see, with your *"own spirit,"* right before *"your own eyes," how the Spirit of God is not in the modern Bible versions.* It will be obvious to your spirit as you read, and compare for *yourself, without the help* or *interference* of the scholars. And guess what? You do not have to be an expert in Greek. You have the English right before you as you compare the English translations. But, before we do this, consider the question of *"which Bible,"* from a *"logical point of view."*

LOGIC tells us that if two particular things are *different*, or *opposite*, they both can't be *right*. It is possible that they both can be *wrong*. It is also possible that one is *right* and one is *wrong. But they both can't be right if they do not agree.* So if one Bible tells us "one thing," and another Bible tells us something completely opposite, or different, they both can't be right, and if one of them happens to be right, or if one of them belongs to God, then the other is a COUNTERFEIT. Let the counterfeit leave your heart and mind, and help a friend to do the same. It is an insult to God to believe that any counterfeit somehow is *accepted* by Him. God is not *intimidated* by the scholars of *"textual criticism."* Neither is God accountable to these scholars.

Look at Proverbs 1:1-5:

"The proverbs of Solomon the son of David, king of Israel; to know wisdom and instruction; to perceive the words of understanding; to receive the instruction of wisdom, justice, and judgment, and equity; to give subtlety to the simple, to the young man knowledge and discretion. A wise man will hear, and will increase learning; and a man of understanding shall attain unto wise counsels."

Will your pastor do that? Will you do that? Will you investigate for yourself the *truth* concerning this important matter of your Bible? Will you hold your pastor responsible for doing the same? After all, the Bible is our rule book for life. If a doctrine does not line up with the Word of God, then it is a doctrine that was made by man. We see this in religion all the time. Religion is man's way of reaching God, but Christianity is God's way of reaching man.

All false religions have one thing in common. They have a system of "works" instead of a system of "faith." The Roman Catholic Church will claim both "faith and works." This is Biblically impossible. Romans 11:6 shows us that God had to choose one or the other. The Bible also shows us in the book of James that our works are an evidence of our faith. Our faith saves us. We do good works *because* we are saved. We do not do good works so that God will save us. If God chose "works" as His system to save us, what percentage of "good works" is needed to make it into heaven?

Your decision is *vital*. Don't think for a minute that you cannot do this. YOU MUST! You have a lot more *leverage* and *influence* than you think. It is a privilege for your pastor to have you as part of God's Church. *You are the one who ultimately pays the bills.* Your pastor works for *God*, on *your behalf*. It is his responsibility to be honest with you. The *truth* is that this *issue* has been *swept* under the rug for some 130 years. We have gone downhill since the Word of God was first attacked in the English Bible. We will continue to move away from God unless *the people take the bull by its horns and reverse the process of using counterfeit Bibles in our churches' pulpits.* Otherwise, life will continue to get worse in America, and our churches will have no *power* to encourage the people of America to *return to God with a genuine repentance/revival.* The unbelieving world is watching us. We must begin this effort by returning to the true Bible. We must focus on this first step. There is no other alternative.

Chapter two

You Just Found Out

Are you over the *shock* yet? How come this issue is not discussed in *Sunday School*? Why do we no longer have well done, respectful *debates*? Why did it take a special effort from someone else other than your *pastor* to find out that something with *the Scriptures in English is drastically wrong*? Sorry that you are just finding out about this problem in your Bible. Isn't the *Bible* the *most important book in our possession*? Is not the *Bible* about *life itself*?

My *pastor* instructs me to read the *Bible* all the time. *The Bible is our final authority in all matters of faith and practice.* How did this get *by us*? Why weren't you presented with both sides of this issue? *Fox News* prides itself on being fair and balanced. They report; you decide. Try asking your pastor to bring in someone to debate the issue of counterfeit Bibles. You will see him dodge the invitation. If I am wrong, please invite me to the debate. It will only happen if you, and the other members of the church, insist upon it.

Surely, your *pastor* does not want you to read a *counterfeit Bible.* Do you think that he does? Does he *really care* about this *issue*? As long as you are *reading* from where he is *preaching*, and as long as it lines up with the *denomination's choice,* and his *alma mater's choice,* then he is comfortable? AND THIS IS OK? Is that what it is supposed to be about? No! *You the sheep must be fed.* You are going to have to take the initiative to study this issue on your own because you will not get any help from your pastor.

The *pastor* has taken the responsibility of leadership in the church, HAS HE NOT? Your *pastor* should be concerned with *all the truth,* especially when it comes to the *Word of God.* He should not be concerned with how much he should backtrack and whether his comfort zones are being disturbed. Truth is being attacked! *The Bible has been attacked since Genesis chapter three, when the devil said, "Yea, hath God said."* A great *lie* has been told by the *devil* and is now being supported by the *modern-day scholars.* God tells us in His Word how HE feels about the subject: look again at these preservation Scriptures. The doctrine of *"preservation"* is no longer preached by most *pastors.* But *"preservation"* is still present in the Bible. It is still a *doctrine in the Bible that God has given to us.* This doctrine is clear through the following verses, among others.

"I will worship toward thy holy temple, and praise thy name for thy loving-kindness, and for thy truth: for thou hast magnified thy word above all thy name." (Psalm 138:2.)

God magnifies His Word above all His Name. We know that His Name is a Name above all Names. He alone is God. God values *His Word* even more than He values *His Name.* He ceases from being God if He sins just one time, so He is not going to write this verse in the Bible for us and not mean it. His Word is the most important thing to Him. God's Word holds up everything that He has ever spoken into existence. If God breaks His Word just one time, the universe will collapse! He will cease from being God.

If God never *"changes,"* then who gave any man the right to *change* the Word that He *holds dear?* Yet, the NIV changes the word "them" to "us" in Psalm 12:6-7, *making only the people to be preserved.* How can the people be preserved without the Word of God? The people are preserved also, because God's Word is preserved. The people cannot be "preserved" without the "Word" being "preserved." The NIV only has this *half right.* The Word that He has spoken and written is the Word that He has given to us. God got it *right* the first time. God sees to it, to preserve His Word for us, because we just mess it up.

The last command that Jesus ever gave us is found in Revelation 22:18-19:

"For I testify unto every man that heareth the words of the prophecy of this book, If any man shall add unto these things, God shall add unto him the plagues that are written in this book: And if any man shall take away from the words of the book of this prophecy, God shall take away his part out of the book of life, and out of the Holy City, and from the things which are written in this book."

When God says that He will take away "his part" out of the book of life, He does not mean salvation. Salvation cannot be lost. He does mean we will lose *"blessings and rewards"* for taking things out of His Word or adding things to His Word. Does your church seem blessed to you?

Consider this verse:

"For verily I say unto you, Till heaven and earth pass, one jot or one tittle shall in no wise pass from the law, till all be fulfilled." (Matt. 5:18.)

Jots and tittles are part of the Hebrew language. Remember, the Lord used the Jews to write and to PRESERVE our Old Testament. The Book of Matthew is written to the Jews. God told the Old Testament priests and scribes not to change one little bit of His Word because God had a "design," for His Word that was all His Own.

A book on "God's design," written by Gail Riplinger, entitled *In Awe of Thy Word,* is highly recommended. Gail Riplinger not only looks at *verses* and *words*, she looks at *letters* as well. I also recommend Dr. Sam Gipp's book, *Gipp's Understandable History of the Bible*. Dr. Gipp covers every angle possible from a *historical perspective* on where we *were* and where we are *now*.

Dr. Gipp also wrote a book entitled *The Answer Book*. In this book Dr. Gipp covers *every subject in this issue,* and renders a biblical answer to every lie ever told by the scholars who skillfully kept certain information *quiet* to the Bible college student. Dr. Gipp's answers to these questions are *factual* and *historically accurate*. These books and more are *must* reading for anyone who is interested in finding out the *truth* concerning this subject. The "answer book" has not been refuted.

This is serious business! God has warned us not to mess with His precious Words of instruction. His Words to us are very important to Him. Remember, He magnifies His Word even above His Name. How can we let the scholars, denominational leaders and most pastors get away with tampering with the Words of God? Every *pastor* must be held accountable to the Lord and to the people for allowing the tampering of God's Word to happen. Every *pastor* must look into this issue, even if it goes against his denominational teaching. He cannot allow himself to be bound, by any authority that goes against God, concerning the Word of God.

The *truth* is that we have been following men. We are fearful to contend for the faith in this issue, because we are intimidated by our *pastor*. We do not want to *rock the boat*. We do not want to cause DIVISION. But what is the opposite of *division*? Is it not *unity*? Who are the people who want to *unify* on the Word of God? Is it not the King James people?

So who is causing the division? The people who do not want the English-speaking people *united* on one preserved Bible are the people who are causing the division. After all, there was only one Bible for *centuries*. The Bible in English was complete. There were no other versions of the Bible that were not saying the same thing. Actually, there should be no such thing as a "version" of the Bible. We either have the Bible in English, or we have something else.

When the English-speaking Christians were united on one Bible, which was in the hands of the people, they were able to discern the doctrinal heresies that arose within the Catholic Church. The Roman Catholic Church dominated church history from 400 A.D. to about 1400 A.D. This time in history was known as the "dark ages." The Roman Catholic Church still discourages the Bible from being in the hands of the common person. She knows that if the Bible was in the hands of the people, with the Holy Spirit interpreting the Scriptures, the people would see her false doctrines very clearly. Catholic doctrines simply are not supported by the Scriptures. We will examine the false doctrines of the Roman Catholic Church perhaps in a later book, the Lord willing. (See the letter in the contents.)

Why have we gone from one perfectly preserved Bible to so much confusion? We let *other* people do our *thinking* for us. We follow our *pastors and college professors* blindly and without question. But we have *no problem* taking God out of the *picture*. Why do we feel *safe* when we offend God? This is very *dangerous*. Our *pastors* are not always following God concerning Bible versions. Our *pastors* are only men. They too are human. Some of our pastors are just *ignorant* concerning this problem because they were not taught correctly by their college professors. On the other hand, most pastors are flat-out *indifferent*. They choose to be *unreachable*. Hopefully, your pastor is open to be *taught*. Hopefully, he is not too *proud*. Have you noticed whether your pastor is arrogant or whether he is teachable?

Many *pastors*, in their sermons, sound good on Sunday morning. One of my board members, Ed Lytle, said, "I am convinced that it is not what most of our pastors are *preaching* that poses a problem to a repentance/revival. I am convinced that the problem of having no revival in the church lies with what most of our pastors are *not preaching*." They are not telling us about the problems that are facing Christians today concerning the diversity of our own Bible and some *other problems* that have not yet been discussed. They are not always "rightly dividing the word of truth."

Doctrine is no longer *valued* by most of our pastors, and neither is it *preached*. *Unity* has become a higher value than *truth*. We know that the Bible warns us of a *false unity* and a *false peace*. But we ignore it anyway. We know that "false unity" and "false peace" will be ushered into this world by the *anti-Christ*. We are to be especially unified in our Bible. But it is in our Bible that we are the most divided.

The most important problem facing Christians today is the issue of the *preserved Word of God in English*. Our Bible is under attack. You must do something about it, because most *pastors* will not address this subject at all, and they will encourage you to do the same. *But you must challenge them to address the issue.* You must bring this issue to the attention of each *member of the church*. You can start with the *board of directors*. For, I am convinced that this is the *number one reason* we do not have a repentance/revival breaking out in the churches of America. We have once again broken the *Word of the Covenant*.

Let's take a look at how much God values HIS WORD. Hopefully, this will move you to challenge your *pastor* to look at this subject anew, with you being equipped and knowing what you are talking about.

Chapter Three

God's View Concerning His Word

We looked at Psalm 138:2 and read that God magnifies His Word even above all His Name. God also takes great pains to preserve His Word. In Psalm 12:6-7 it says:

"The words of the Lord are pure words: As silver tried in a furnace of earth, purified seven times. Thou shalt keep them, O Lord, Thou shalt preserve them from this generation for ever."

What God Himself will preserve for us, according to the Scriptures, are HIS WORDS. He thinks that it is very important for us to have HIS WORDS.

Let us learn from the *"Bible Itself"* concerning Josiah's Reform. King Josiah brought Israel back to the "Word of the Covenant." In a nutshell, when Josiah became King, the people were not using "The Word of God." They allowed the Word to get out of their sight until Josiah brought the Word of the Covenant back to them. Read II Kings chapter 22 & II Kings chapter 23. Look at II Kings 22:9-13 in particular.

"And Shaphan the scribe came to the king, and brought the king word again, and said, Thy servants have gathered

the money that was found in the house, and have delivered it into the hand of them that do the work, that have the oversight of the house of the Lord.

And Shaphan the scribe, shewed the king, saying, Hilkiah the priest hath delivered me a book. And Shaphan read it before the king.

And it came to pass, when the king had heard the words of the book of the law, that he rent his clothes. And the king commanded Hilkiah the priest, and Ahikam the son of Shaphan, and Achbor the son of Michaiah, and Shaphan the scribe, and Asahiah a servant of the king's saying,

"Go ye, enquire of the Lord for me, and for the people, and for all Judah, concerning the words of this book that is found: for great is the wrath of the Lord that is kindled against us, because our fathers have not hearkened unto the words of this book, to do according unto all that which is written concerning us."

Later on you will read that Josiah gathered up all of his *leadership*. He instructed them that they must *return to the Word of the Covenant*. As a result of Josiah's obedience in "keeping the Word of God," *great reform* came about in Israel for as long as the people obeyed the Word of God. Remember, Josiah was a very young king at this time, so don't say you cannot do anything about this situation. Great blessings and revival in our churches will come to us as well, if we get back to the Word of the Covenant.

No modern scholar was ever authorized by God to be a *corrector of God and His Word*. No man can ever correct God, for God is perfect. No modern Bible scholar can hold a candle to what God has already written and preserved in English. Not a single post 1881 Bible has proven to be better then what God already produced in English, starting in 1380 with John Wycliffe. This includes the *lies that the modern Bibles are easier to read and to understand*. It will be shown later in this book that there are *more hard words versus easy words in the NIV, than in the KJB.*

Think about God's effort in writing the Bible. God went through a lot to give us HIS WORD. He has used over 40 different authors over some 1,500 years to get His Words into our hands. He paid a great price to reveal HIMSELF to us. In English, He started the process using *John Wycliffe* and *William Tyndale*. The former was vilified by the Roman Catholics, and the latter was burnt at the stake, for translating the Bible into English. Remember, John Wycliffe used the Old Latin Bible of about 147 A.D., and that version should not be confused with the Latin Vulgate of the Catholic Church that was written by Jerome in

395 A.D. Therefore, Wycliffe started off with the Antiochan Manuscripts that are not used by Westcott and Hort. These manuscripts were not used by the Roman Catholic Church. The Scriptures were not in the hands of the people for about 1,000 years. Wycliffe also used the corrupted manuscripts because he had no choice in dealing with the Catholic Church. Erasmus Greek text was not available to Wycliffe at the time of his translation.

God used Miles Coverdale, to John Rogers, to the Great Bible and on to the Geneva Bible. All of the Bibles in English, written before the King James, came from the same preserved manuscripts. There was no change of text. They all used the preserved manuscripts found in Antioch Syria.

Surely God kept His Word when He promised that the Bible would be *purified seven times*. All the aforementioned Bibles were precursors to the King James Bible, which was the *eighth* Bible in English. There were 7 precursor Bibles before the King James Bible. The Bible was purified 7 times just like it said it would be in Psalm 12:6-7. Howbeit that 7 is the perfect number of God. He used 7 *universal languages* in the course of history, and He purified the English line of Bibles 7 times before His final product in English which was the King James Bible.

Those 7 languages were: *Hebrew, Aramaic, Greek, Syrian, Latin, German, and finally, English.* Can a Josiah of the church be found in today's world? Will any significant leader make a call for the church to return to the "word of the covenant?" We all cry out for revival, but we do not know the price that must be paid for that revival. If we do know the price that must be paid for revival, we do not seem to be strong enough in our will to pay that price. We must begin with our "personal repentance." It's me, it's me, it's me oh God, standing in the need of prayer. My youth kids sing this song and believe it. Do you?

We can see *God's design* in His use of the number seven. Why didn't He stop at *five? Everything that God has done in His Word has meaning.* All of God's "design" coordinates across the board with every word and every letter. God's Word is perfect. There are no mistakes or contradictions. The textual critics will point to an apparent contradiction. What they are pointing to are "problem text" that have an answer for when we check "Scripture with Scripture." There were editions and corrections within the *purification process*, but there was never a *change in the text*. Dr. Sam Gipp writes further on this point in his book, *The Answer Book*. Dr. Gipp's book will help you to have an answer for

51

every bit of *misinformation* that has been given by the modern day scholars, concerning the King James Bible.

In order to *justify themselves,* the enemies of the preserved Word of God, *who know better*, have come up with many *false statements* that do not *justify* their changing of the Bible. But if you study yourself to be approved of God and investigate, you will have every question answered with truth and accuracy. All you have to do is be willing to study. But arrogance is the most common trait of rebellion. Many college students have an *arrogant attitude* concerning their education. They have become *"puffed up."* But they do not know *both sides of the issue* because their *education was biased.* Perhaps, they are just not seeking the truth.

God didn't have to *reveal Himself* to us through His Word. But He knew we would never make it in this world, unless He wrote things down for us, and PRESERVED His writings by Himself. He could not trust *man* when it came to *preserving His Word through time.* He could *foresee* modern day scholarship. Man is not qualified to correct God. But many *scholars* and *universities* have corrected God's Word to the *demise* of the *people.* There was no need to correct God. He is still perfect in all that "He is" and in all that "He does." Malachi 3:6 says:

"For I am the Lord, I change not; therefore ye sons of Jacob are not consumed."

They led the people to believe that they were only changing the *Elizabethan dialect. But modern scholars changed much more than just the Elizabethan "thee's and thou's,* which they claimed to be changing. But note: God does not want us to change the thee's and thou's anyway. (See I Samuel chapter 9.)

An attitude that seeks to correct God will stifle any repentance/revival that could break out in the age of Laodicea. God will not visit us unless we show that we care about His Word. *Are you up to the task to change this situation?* Do you care about God's Word? Here is more instruction from the Bible itself concerning the Word of God. Amos 3:8 says:

"The lion hath roared, who will not fear? The Lord God hath spoken, who can but prophesy?"

The fire has to burn in you, the average Christian, if we are to turn this problem around, and give God a chance to visit us in a real GENUINE REVIVAL. Remember the words of Jeremiah the prophet who said in Jeremiah 20:9:

"Then I said, I will not make mention of him, nor speak any more in his name.

But His Word was in mine heart as a burning fire shut up in my bones, and I was weary with forbearing, and I could not stay."

Another preservation verse says this in Matthew 24:35:

"Heaven and earth shall pass away, but my words shall not pass away."

No matter what *man* tries to do to destroy the Word of God he will not be able to succeed. The Word of God will always be available to us by the hand of God *Himself*. He will see to it that we have His Word, if we want to use it. *But will we use it?*

It is just as bad to have the Word of God available to us and NOT USE IT, then to simply NOT have the Word of God at ALL. Thanks to God Himself, we do have His Word. *It has been perfectly preserved through time and it is available to us today.* But, *"we the people"* are no longer using the preserved Word of God because our pastors have us on one of the 200 or more *counterfeits*. Even these counterfeits do not agree with each other. The devil will destroy the people's *faith* in the Word of God if we let this happen. This is why the *church*, in general, has lost its power. The Bible is our "final authority." Take a look at this next verse in Proverbs 30:5-6:

"Every word of God is pure: He is a shield unto them that put their trust in Him. Add thou not unto His words, lest He reprove thee, and thou be found a liar."

Don't we trust that God has kept His Words PURE? Why would a *perfect God*, not *perfectly preserve*, the Word that He loves, for us? Would He let His Word be lost so that we can have an EXCUSE? The Bible tells us that we are *without excuse*. (See Romans 1:20.)

We are without EXCUSE because God wrote down for us all that He wants us to know. He was going to make sure we had it in *writing*. No one can say that they didn't know what God expected of them. They may not have read His precepts, or obeyed them, but they can never say they did not have the chance to do so. God's Word was always available, so *all the more reason why our pastors should not mislead the sheep.*

When the sheep are put on a counterfeit Bible by their *pastor*, the sheep are not "moved" and they have little "power" because they are on a "dull sword." This "dull sword" does not cut to the *"bone and marrow."* The preserved Word of God is a *"sharp sword."* It cuts through *"bone and marrow."* (Hebrews 4:12)

As Dr. Sam Gipp says in his book, *Gipp's Understandable History of the Bible*, speaking about God's Word, "Why eat HAMBURGER when you can have a

STEAK?"[15] Why a *"dull sword"* instead of a *"sharp sword?"* What do you think this has done to our pastors' preaching? The weak preaching of our pastors will not change our culture.

The pastor of your church has a great responsibility. He is the main person who will preach the Word of God to you. You have a right to be concerned, if he is not preaching the Word of God. Some people do not read their Bibles at all. Perhaps they are not sure as to which Bible is God's Word? In this case it is even more important for you to encourage your pastor to preach and to teach from God's Bible and not his *Alma Mater's* Bible. But, how will you know where the true Word of God is to be found if your pastor does not *address* the issue? *If you do not take the time to address this issue for yourself,* you will never know where the *true Word of God can be found.*

You might have asked a question or two and you might have gotten a *"flimsy explanation."* In the end, the preserved Word of God always seems to get put down *unjustly* and *incorrectly.* The King James Bible is always wrong when it comes to the true Bible. Yet, when you and your pastor are discussing the King James Bible face to face, *comparative verses* are never being *read with the eyes.* It is always a *"verbal conversation"* with your pastor doing most of the talking. He always gets the last word, while you are left to feel stupid and uneducated. After all, he is the pastor and you are just a layman. Yet for over 250 years, all of the English-speaking people were united on one Bible and the pastors of the church were under the same authority as you.

The Protestant Reformation of 1517 survived its separation from the Roman Catholic Church because of the "preserved Word of God." The Protestants and the Baptists (the latter existed before the reformation) were delivered from the bondage of the Roman Catholic Church. The greatest revivals in Christian history were when the people had the preserved Word of God in English.

Now, however, we have not had a genuine renewal in the Christian Church for over 130 years. Our preaching has no *power* to close down the *bars* and the *prostitute houses.* Casinos are being built all over the country. But when a true *revival* comes to us, it will make an *indelible mark on history.* Something big will *change* in the way we *conduct our lives.* How can there be revival without repentance?

The Bible has the power to change our *culture.* Wouldn't it be great if "we the

---

15. Gipp, *Gipp's Understandable History of the Bible*, p. 6.

people" had the power to overturn Roe versus Wade? The church must unite on the preserved Word of God and regain its power, in order for a repentance/ revival to become a reality. While the Marxist Democratic Party promotes the killing of babies, the Republican party is more interested in making money on the abortion issue instead of winning the right of the unborn to live. So we must depend on God to win this battle for us. He wants to use you, but we must allow Him to have the pre-eminence in our lives. He can only guide us from His preserved Word.

The Muslims are united on the Koran. The devil does not disturb their Bible, because he is not threatened by it. Yet, we let the devil get away with disturbing our Bible. If we were at the table with the Muslims, talking about peace, they would tear up our Bible, because the different versions contradict themselves. They are never completely the same, and our own precious Christian doctrines are attacked within our own Bible versions.

To put ourselves in that position is absurd. We lose our *"sharp sword,"* because we have traded our *"sharp sword"* for a *"dull sword,"* that no longer *"moves us."* If our Bible no longer *"moves us"* when we read it, how can it ever move the Muslims to receive Jesus as their Saviour, when, and if, they check our Bible for the truth? Don't be fooled by false teaching. The Muslim religion is no different than any other religion that has man reaching up to find God, rather then allowing God to find man by His reaching down to us. Jesus Christ saved us, because He was God, who manifest Himself in the flesh. Who is the author of confusion? The answer is found in our preserved Bible. God is not the author of *confusion*. I Corinthians 14:33.

The Bible tells us these things about Jesus in John 14:6:

"Jesus saith unto him, I am the way, the truth, and the life: No man cometh unto the Father, but by me."

We see from this verse that we have "one way," "one truth," and "one life." So how come we have *"many Bibles?"*

In Ephesians 4:5 the Bible says that there is:

"One Lord, one faith, one baptism."

So once again, how come we have many Bibles that are consistently *not saying the same thing?* Isn't Jesus the same *Yesterday, Today, and Forever?*

Have you and your pastor ever done a *comparative study together?* Hopefully, the blind are not leading the blind when it comes to this issue. If you never had the chance to see this *truth for yourself,* then you are taking your *pastor* at his word, just because he is *your pastor.* Yet, you were never instructed by God to follow a man that is not following God. You have to know whether the Bible your pastor is using is the Bible that God gave you, and wants you to have and to use. Or, if the Bible from which your *pastor* is preaching is a COUNTERFEIT.

The NIV and other modern Bible versions have no use for the doctrine of preservation. Why would they? They have butchered the Word of God in many places in the name of "textual criticism." They have criticized God. I wonder how God feels when scholars try to correct Him. There is no regard, as to how God feels on the part of the scholars, whatsoever. They were never as careful with the Scriptures as the Jews were with the Old Testament.

The Levites, the priests, and the scribes were in charge of preserving the Old Testament Scriptures. There are numerous Old Testament verses that testify to this. The Jews did a great job in preserving God's Word. If the scribes made one mistake in copying the Scriptures they would painstakingly start all over again until the copies were perfect. In Matt. 5:18 the Bible says:

"For verily I say unto you, Till heaven and earth pass, one jot or one tittle shall in no wise pass from the law, till all be fulfilled."

Who do you think helped them to preserve the Scriptures? It was God Himself who made sure that His Word would be preserved. I suppose when all is "fulfilled" and we are in heaven, we will have a fulfilled knowledge of the Bible. But God knew that He needed to write the Scriptures out for us so that we can know His precepts while on earth. God knows that we will use, as an excuse, that we did not know our condition before Him. But we have no excuse if we miss His plan for our Salvation and His plan to know His Word. Dr. Gipp tells us in his book, *The Answer Book,* that "there is no *inspiration* without *preservation.*"[16] Why would God inspire His Scriptures and then have no part in preserving them?

How can you, the average Christian, who is a member of the flock, know for sure that you have God's Word when you read the Bible? How can you be convinced within yourself that the Bible you have, and love, is the Bible that truly belongs to God? Can you really know? *Yes, you can.* But you must have faith in God's ability to preserve His Word. You can have complete confidence that the preserved words of God in English are available to you today and

---

16. Gipp. *The Answer Book.* (Miamitown, Ohio: Daystar Publishing, 1989 or 2003) p. 19.

placed right into your hands. In Psalm 119:89 it says:

"For ever, O Lord, thy word is settled in heaven."

Let's do a comparative study and see with our *"spirit"* not just our *"intellect,"* *where the Spirit of God is present concerning His Word.*

There is nothing like seeing this right before your eyes. Look with your Spirit, and let God's Spirit testify to the truth. The Holy Spirit promised to guide you into God's truth, if you let Him do this for you. Put all of your bias away and study this for yourself. God's Spirit will guide you. The Holy Spirit in you will bear witness to the truth. Your scholar friends are not able to interfere with the Holy Spirit that lives within you. Consider this verse when the modern day scholars talk about a "dynamic equivalent." In Matt. 4:4 God says:

"But he answered and said, It is written, Man shall not live by bread alone, but by every <u>word</u> that proceedeth out of the <u>mouth</u> of <u>God</u>"

However, a "dynamic equivalent" is really saying this:

"But he answered and said, It is written, Man shall not live by bread alone, but by every <u>thought</u> that proceeds out of the <u>head</u> of <u>God</u>."

By the way, in Luke 4:4 where this same verse is also quoted, the last part of this verse is completely omitted.

The preserved Word of God is a "word for word" translation. The modern Bible translations are only a "dynamic equivalent." Why believe a "dynamic equivalent" when you have the "dynamic" right in your hands?

David prayed a prayer in Psalms 119:43: He said:

"And take not the word of truth utterly out of my mouth; for I have hoped in thy judgments."

Let the different Bibles speak for themselves. If we were to put this issue on trial, the prosecution would prove that the post 1881 Bibles from Westcott and Hort and the Nestle Aland texts are counterfeit. Let's prove this case. *You be the judge.*

Chapter Four

A Comparative Study from a Spiritual View (See for Yourself)

Jesus Falls From Grace

Isaiah 14:12 will show that the NIV makes our Saviour **Jesus Christ to fall from heaven, instead of Lucifer the devil**. See this with your own eyes as you study. Look up Isaiah 14:12. Note: *In the higher degrees of "freemasonry,"* the masons make *Lucifer to be Lord. That is exactly what the NIV does. This is perfectly in line with the Freemasons who are driving the *New World Order*. How can we doubt this connection?

KJB - *"How art thou fallen from heaven, O Lucifer, son of the morning! How art thou cut down to the ground, which didst weaken the nations!"*

NIV – *"How you have fallen from heaven, O Morning Star, son of the dawn! You have been cast down to the earth, you who once laid low the nation."*

There is no debate whatsoever to the Biblical Fact that Jesus Christ is the *MORNING STAR*. Both the NIV and the KJB verify this in Revelation 22:16 and in Revelation 2:28. The NIV drops the word *"Lucifer"* and adds the word *"morning star"* in Isaiah 14:12. The NIV makes *Jesus*

59

fall instead of *Lucifer*. What spirit wants this to happen right in God's own *Bible*? How is your *spirit* talking to you now?

All you have to have is one verse shown to be wrong in Spirit for you to be sure that a COUNTERFEIT can be spotted. See how Satan and apostate scholars have coyly gotten this in your Bible? They got this in your Bible right under your pastor's nose. Shame on your church *pastor*, for allowing the information of a counterfeit Bible, to hurt you. On this point alone, you should put down your modern Bible and never use it again!

This is one of two accounts in the Bible that give us the story of Satan falling from Heaven. The other is in Ezekiel 31:16. What Spirit wants our Saviour to fall in His own Bible? Only the Spirit of the devil, and those who follow the devil, want our Saviour to fall in His own Bible instead of Lucifer. *The truth is being exchanged for a lie.* (See Romans 1:25.) This is not only a *PERVERSION OF THE BIBLE,* it is *BLASPHEMY*!

Now look at Isaiah 14:15 and see that the NIV sentences Lucifer to the *"grave"* instead of to *"hell."* In some other verses we will see that words like *"devil and hell,"* have been changed to *"demon and hades."* A demon in the grave, or a demon in hades, is not as threatening as a devil in hell. Hades is the Greek word for hell. You cannot use the Greek word itself as part of the text in the translation. Hades sounds like a vacation spot in the Caribbean. What Spirit does not want us to think of hell as something that is severe? What is so special about the grave? We will all go to the grave someday. But those who receive Jesus as their personal Saviour will not go to hell.

Jesus Sins

Now let's see how the NIV makes our Saviour Jesus to SIN. Look up Matt. 5:22A. Compare and see which Bible has the true Spirit of God. We will look at just the first half of this verse.

KJB - *"But I say unto you, That whosoever is angry with his brother, without a cause, shall be in danger of the judgment."*

NIV - *"But I tell you that anyone who is angry with his brother will be subject to judgment."*

The NIV leaves out "without a cause." Anger is an *"emotion."* Many times *"anger"* will certainly lead to *"sin."* But sometimes, anger is *"justified."* The Bible tells us to:

"Be angry and sin not."

This verse is found in Eph. 4:26. When anger is *justified*, it is not *sin*. There is such a thing as *"righteous anger."* If we go by the NIV verse as being God's *truth*, then Jesus sinned when He overturned the money changers in John 2:15, because Jesus was angry when He overturned those stone tables. He did not just tiptoe up to the money exchangers and politely ask them to leave. He made a *"scourge of small cords,"* and *"drove them out."*

The Muslims would have a field day with this verse in our Bible if we told them that the NIV was God's Word. We can no longer make the case to the Muslims that our Bible is perfectly preserved and that it comes from God. We have to show them the Word of God from the Bible that was given to us by God. The Muslims can look at our 200 different versions of the Bible and point out all the inconsistencies. This is laughable.

See how leaving a phrase out, or changing a word, can change *meaning*? Jesus just lost His perfect power because the NIV shows Him to sin when He was angry with the money changers. But, every Christian knows that Jesus *never sinned.* In the NIV and other modern Bible versions though, there will always be the question as to whether Jesus crossed the line by being angry with the *"money changers."* According to the NIV in this verse, Jesus was angry with his brother and was in danger of the judgment.

Also in Luke 2:22, the NIV uses the word *"their"* instead of *"her"* concerning *"purification."* Jesus never sinned, so He does not need to be purified. But Mary, the earthly mother of Jesus, had to be purified after giving birth, as was the custom of the Jews recorded in Leviticus chapter 12. You will never hear a Catholic priest preach from Luke 2:22.

If you change *"words,"* you will change *"meaning."* If you change *"meaning,"* you will change *"doctrine."* If you change *"doctrine,"* you will change *"theology."* If you change *"theology,"* you change *"belief."* If you change *"belief,"* you will change *"actions."* You will change the way you *believe* and *act.* What a great strategy of the *devil.* If I were the *devil,* I would try to change the *Words of God.* That is exactly what the modern day scholars have done. *We the people,* let them get away with it. This should be upsetting to everyone who loves and defends the Word of God.

We need to take our King James Bible with us to the table if we ever discuss truth with the Muslims, Atheists, Hindus, Buddhist, and to those who preach *"another gospel,"* like the Roman Catholics. None of the aforementioned believe that we must go through Jesus Christ to be saved. The Catholics say that they believe this, but then they provide a *"false system of beliefs,"* as to *"how"* we are to be *saved*. The Catholic Jesus is not the Jesus of the Bible. The Catholic system is not a *"biblical"* system. There needs to be a *"revolution"* concerning the subject of our *"changed"* Bible. We need a Bible *"tea party."*

Jesus Comes from an Unruly Geneology

Now, let's see how Jesus comes from an *"unruly genealogy"* in the NIV. This next verse is a *"direct opposite"* of the Word of God. Look up Hosea 11:12:

KJB – *"Ephraim compasseth me about with lies, and the house of Israel with deceit: but Judah yet ruleth with God, and is faithful with the saints."*

NIV – *"Ephraim has surrounded me with lies, the house of Israel with deceit. And Judah is unruly against God, even against the faithful Holy one."*

Here is a verse that is completely opposite of the Word of God. The NIV makes Jesus come from an *"unruly genealogy."*

Jesus comes from the Tribe of Judah, in the line of David. Mary's genealogy traces back to Nathan who is the son of David. This is the *"royal"* line in Jesus' genealogy. Even Joseph is traced back to David through his son Solomon. This is the *"legal"* line in Jesus' genealogy. Judah was blessed of God, because Joshua and Caleb gave a good report on the taking of the land of Canaan, (The 14th chapter of the book of Numbers.) The other 10 tribes of Israel, or the Northern Kingdom, were not blessed. What Spirit wants Jesus to come from an *"unruly genealogy?"*

Judah was not perfect, but God maintained His promise to bless Judah because of the faith of Joshua and Caleb. Hosea 11:12 in the KJB also maintains God's promise. But the NIV destroys this promise, the same Spirit that makes Jesus to *"fall"* and to *"sin,"* makes Jesus come from an *"unruly genealogy."* Doesn't the NIV like the "blessed line" of David, into which our *Saviour* was born?

What is your Spirit saying to you about this right now? Isn't God's Bible showing itself to be *"right and true?"* You should feel the *"peace"* in your spirit right now. If you have read thus far, you can see, that what God wrote for us and preserved is consistent across the board. All we need is *"one verse"* showing us something to be wrong in our Bible. If one verse is *"wrong,"* then the Bible is *"errant."* You were just shown three things to be *"wrong"* in the counterfeits, but there is more. Let's look at Isaiah 59:19:

The Enemy is Coming, Raise Up a Standard Against Him

KJB – *"So shall they fear the name of the Lord from the west, and His glory from the rising of the sun. When the enemy shall come in like a flood, the Spirit of the Lord shall lift up a standard against him."*

NIV – *"From the west, men will fear the name of the Lord, and from the rising of the sun, they will revere His glory. For He will come like a pent-up flood, that the breath of the Lord drives along."*

The NIV uses the pronoun "He" instead of the word, *"enemy."* If you re-read the NIV verse, you will be led to believe that the pronoun *"He"* refers to the *"Lord."* In the NIV the Lord is the one who is coming. But in the *true Word of God,* this verse is talking about the coming of the *"enemy."* The reason this verse talks about the coming of the *"enemy,"* is that God will *"raise up a standard against the enemy."* The NIV completely takes the *"raising of the standard out of the verse."* How come? Doesn't the devil want us to be aware of his presence in our lives? Is the devil afraid that the people will *"raise up a standard"* against him?

The NIV says:

"The breath of the Lord drives along,"

Is that the *"pent-up flood,"* or the *"enemy"*? The NIV is not clear. What *spirit* wants Jesus to *"fall," "sin," "come from an unruly genealogy,"* and have no *"standard against the enemy?"* What SPIRIT wants Jesus coming in a verse that is about the *"presence of the enemy?"*

The Confused Mark of the Beast

Now let's look how the changing of just one letter can bring confusion concerning the *"mark of the beast."* Read Revelation 13:16. (This error can become a very dangerous situation for those who *believe*, and for those who are *left* in the tribulation.)

KJB – *"And he causeth all, both small and great, rich and poor, free and bond, to receive a mark in their right hand, or in their foreheads."*

NIV – *"He also forced everyone, small and great, rich and poor, free and slave, to receive a mark on his right hand or on his forehead."*

You might be saying right now, so what is the big deal? Boy, how picky can one get? What is wrong with this? But watch how the changing of the letter *"i"* for an *"o"* will bring much confusion to the Christian concerning the taking of the *"mark of the beast."*

Early in 2002 a very interesting article appeared in several newspapers, including the Canton, Ohio, Repository. This article, reported that a Florida technology company was poised to ask the government for permission to market a first-ever computer ID chip that could be embedded beneath a person's skin. The chip would be used in airports, nuclear power plants and other high security facilities. The immediate benefits could be a closer-to-foolproof security system. But privacy advocates had warned that the chip could lead to encroachments on civil liberties.[17]

The chip drew attention from several religious groups. Theologian and author Terry Cook said he was concerned that the identification chip could be the *"mark of the beast."* The *"mark of the beast,"* will be an identifying mark that all people will be forced to wear just before the end times according to the Bible. Theologians were consulted, and several of them appeared on the Religious television program the "700 Club" to assure the viewers that the chip didn't fit the Biblical description of the *"mark"* because the chip was going *under the skin* and hidden from view.

But, let's take a look at this. It will certainly make a difference as to what Bible version Pat Robertson and the theologians used. If they are not using the King James Bible to access this situation, then scores of people who trust them can be misled into taking the *"mark of the beast."* Go back and read the two verses once again, and notice that one Bible uses the word *"IN"* and the other Bible uses the word *"ON."*

The team of theologians concluded that there was nothing to worry about because the "mark of the beast" was going "ON" the right hand and the forehead and *this chip* was going "IN" the right hand and forehead. Pat Robertson and the team of theologians concluded the "don't worry" instruction because they were using a Bible version other than the *"King James."* The modern Bible versions are the Bibles that say *"ON."* The true Word of God says *"IN."* *IN* the right hand or IN the forehead is where this chip is going to go. I would be concerned whether the chip was going "in or on."

---

17. Ramstack, Tom. (Apr. 15, 2002.) Firm seeks FDA approval for human microchip implants; the VeriChip is another sign that Sept. 11 has catapulted the effort to secure America into a realm with uncharted possibilities — and possible unintended consequences. *Insight on the News* (online magazine). (Referring to the February 26, 2002 article "Human Computer Chip Studied" in <http://www.usatoday.com/news/nation/2002/02/26/chip.htm> (Accessed June 22, 2011), the Feb. 28, 2002 Washington Time article "Firm seeks FDA approval for human chip implants: Voluntary use planned for medical data, identification ," etc.)

Satan changed just one letter through so-called modern day Bible scholars…
an "o" for an "i" so that scores of people can be deceived in taking the *"mark of
the beast."* This got the approval of our *Christian theologians?* All the *scholars*
and *pastors* who want to tell people that the issue of Bible versions is not worth
fighting over have got to answer this question. Will the *"mark of the beast,"* be
"IN" the right hand or forehead, or *"ON"* the right hand or forehead? The chip is
going *"IN"* the right hand or forehead, and it sounds like the *"mark of the beast,"*
to me. Thank God we Christians will be raptured up before the Tribulation.

What does this sound like to you? Do you want to take the chip and take a
chance? These theologians said that this will be okay. Are you going to *spiritually*
trust the version of the Bible that they use? What *spirit* wants Jesus to:

Fall

Sin

Come from an unruly genealogy.

Have the Lord coming in place of the enemy.

Have no standard against the enemy.

What spirit wants to bring confusion concerning the Mark of the Beast?

In this chapter, I have looked at 5 *"spiritual,"* not *"intellectual"* reasons, why we
should identify the *modern Bibles,* put out after 1881 as *COUNTERFEIT.* They
do not show the *"Spirit of God."* They show *"another spirit."* Consider how God
warns us in Jeremiah 5:1-3 to return to the TRUTH.

*"Run ye to and fro through the streets of Jerusalem, and see now, and know, and
seek in the broad places thereof, if ye can find a man, if there be any that seeketh
the truth; and I will pardon it. And though they say, the Lord liveth; surely they
swear falsely. O Lord, are not thine eyes upon the truth? thou hast consumed
them, but they have refused to receive correction: they have made their faces
harder than a rock; they have refused to return."*

Do you refuse to *return*? What about your pastor? Will he return to the
"preserved Word of God?" With your help, maybe he will. Don't think for one
minute that you cannot help him change his position. You can do it with the
help of God. If you do not do it, it will not get done. *You should stop calling
for a revival to happen.* God will not be able to visit us. It is disobedient if we
continue to break his *last command.*

How many verses will this book need, to convince you that something wrong is going on in your Bible? We should only need one wrong verse before we realize that our Bible is no longer inerrant when it comes to the counterfeits. The Spirit of God versus the Spirit of Error is found in I John 4:6:

"We are of God: He that knoweth God heareth us; he that is not of God heareth not us. Hereby, know we the Spirit of truth, and the Spirit of error."

Are you, the reader, one who, *"knows God?"* Or are you, the reader, one who is, *"not of God and who hears not?"* You can know in your *spirit* what is *true* and what is *not true.* You do not need your *pastor* to see this, and you do not have to be a *"Greek scholar,"* to see this. You just need the *Holy Spirit* speaking to your *heart.* What is He saying?

Now, let's look at the *"doctrinal problems"* imposed on us by modern Bible scholars. The next two chapters will point out several *doctrines* that have been changed in our Bible. Hopefully, your *"intellect"* will pick up where your *"spirit"* has left off.

Chapter Five

Doctrinal Problems in the Counterfeits

"All Scripture is given by inspiration of God, and is profitable for doctrine, for reproof, for correction, for instruction in righteousness." (II Tim. 3:16.)

Notice that the first word listed in this verse among the four reasons why God gave us His inspired Word was *doctrine. Doctrine is what we believe as Christians. The tenants of our very faith are rooted in doctrine.* A *"cult"* becomes a *"cult"* because it does not adhere to a *certain doctrine of the Christian faith.* For example, the Jehovah Witnesses do not believe that *"Jesus is God."* If Jesus is not God, He cannot *forgive our sins.* Only God can forgive our sins. The doctrine of the Deity of Jesus Christ is *central to our faith.* This doctrine says that Jesus Christ is 100% God and 100% Man. The Jehovah Witnesses deny this doctrine.

Let's examine each and every *doctrine* that is important to our faith as Christians. And let us see how the NIV and other counterfeit Bibles, either omit, delete, or change in some way, what we as Christians have always believed to be a doctrine of our faith.

Let's start with the most important doctrine, which

happens to be *Salvation*. The very reason that Jesus came down to earth was to save us, because we could not save ourselves from sin.

Salvation

The whole bottom line of the Bible, and the very reason why God took the time to reveal Himself to us through His Word, is to SAVE US.

"For God so loved the world, that He gave His only begotten Son, that whosoever believeth in Him should not perish, but have everlasting life." (John 3:16.)

Do you know that the NIV and other modern Bibles even mess this verse up? Look it up now and see if you can figure out how they lie to you in this verse. Later in the book, it will be shown why the rendering of this verse in most modern Bibles is wrong.

If the whole Bible can be summed up in just one verse, *this is the verse*. God does not want us to go to HELL. Since we cannot *save ourselves*, God had to visit us in *"human form,"* shed His *OWN* blood on the cross, and give us a *"free will"* choice to *receive* His free gift to be *saved*. (This is the provision of God.) The alternative is to choose Hell, if we do not want to be *saved*.

We cannot earn this free gift by being good, or by doing good works, or by keeping the law, or by doing some sacrament. Not even our holiness will save us. If we sin just one time, which we all have done, then we deserve to be *eternally separated from God*.

"For the wages of sin is death, but the gift of God is eternal life through Jesus Christ our Lord." (Romans 6:23.)

Also, in Isaiah 59:2 it says:

"But your iniquities have separated between you and your God, and your sins have hid his face from you that he will not hear."

God could have given to us whatever SALVATION SYSTEM HE WANTED! If it pleased God to give us a system that had us 51% GOOD, and only 49% BAD, and this would take us *through to heaven*, then He could have done just that, and given us that system. But even in this system of *WORKS*, if we were 99% GOOD, and only 1% BAD, God would not be able to tolerate the 1% BAD in us, because He cannot tolerate sin in any *form, percentage, or manifestation*. That is what PERFECTION does to somebody. Since *God is perfect*, just *one* sin separates us from God for all eternity.

So it would seem that God had a problem. What was He going to do to save us, since we could not save ourselves? What system was He going to use to put this into motion? Romans 11:6 gives us insight into this question. What system was God going to choose to save us? Here is what it says:

"And if by grace, then is it no more of works: otherwise grace is no more grace. But if it be of works then is it no more grace: otherwise work is no more work."

What this is saying is that *"works"* and *"grace"* are like *"oil"* and *"water."* When it comes to *Salvation*, the two cannot mix. God had to choose either one or the other of these two possible systems to save us. Which system did He choose according to the Bible? This question is answered in Ephesians 2:8-9:

"For by grace are ye saved through faith; and that not of yourselves: it is the gift of God: not of works, lest any man should boast."

God chose the system that HE HIMSELF INVENTED to SAVE US. This system of Salvation that God chose puts all the impetus on Himself. He had to *appease* and *satisfy Himself* concerning our sinful, fallen condition. "WORKS" WAS NOT THE SYSTEM THAT SATISFIED GOD. God put Himself on the spot. He became sin for us and died on a cross, while shedding His OWN blood. In this God was satisfied in Himself, as long as we make the decision to *receive this free gift.* We have to *take it, claim it,* and *possess* this free gift for *ourselves*, with a heart and mind decision. Look at John 1:12:

"But as many as received him, to them gave he power to become the sons of God, even to them that believe on his name."

The simple heart and mind decision to receive Jesus Christ as our personal Saviour, makes us righteous in the *eyes of God*. He likes this deal. Boy, did we dodge a bullet. Don't we all deserve hell? Let's take a look at two words, *"grace"* and *"mercy."* It has been said that *"mercy"* is not getting what you do deserve to get, and *"grace"* is getting what you do not deserve to get. We deserve hell, but we can all choose heaven. Which one do you want?

There are many other verses in the Bible that show us, plainly, how to BE SAVED. They all work and coordinate together to show the simplicity of the system that God chose to use. The true Roman Road is as follows. These verses must be fully understood for us to be saved. In Romans 3:23 it says:

"For all have sinned and come short of the glory of God."

In Romans 6:23 it says:

"For the wages of sin is death; but the gift of God is eternal life through Jesus Christ our Lord."

In Romans 5:8 it says:

"But God commendeth his love toward us, in that, while we were yet sinners, Christ died for us."

In Romans 10:9-10, it says:

"That if thou shalt confess with thy mouth the Lord Jesus, and shalt believe in thine heart that God hath raised him from the dead, thou shalt be saved."

In Romans 10:13 it says:

"For whosoever shall call upon the name of the Lord shall be saved."

I didn't see anything about *"good works,"* when it comes to our *justification*. I did not see anything about *"praying to Mary."* I did not see anything in these verses about *"having to go to purgatory."* I did not see anything about having to *"receive Jesus in a wafer."* I did not see anything in these verses about *"obeying the law of the Old Testament."* There is nothing in these verses about *"going to a catholic mass."*

I did not see anything in these verses about *"confessing my sins to a priest."* (There is no biblical authorization for a *"mass,"* or for a *"priest,"* in the New Testament.) Read Hebrews chapters 8-10. I did not see anything about a *"scapular."* (Anyone who was never a Roman Catholic will have to look this one up.)

Concerning those who believe in baptismal regeneration, I see no verse that equates *Baptism* or the *Lord's Supper,* or *circumcision*, as being connected to *justification*. All the verses connected to both the Lord's Supper and to baptism have to do with *Sanctification*. In obedience we do these things because we *are* saved. We do not do these things to get saved. Failure to do a command of the Lord, will cost you *"blessings and rewards,"* but you cannot *lose* your Salvation, once you receive Christ with your heart and believe.

The theological subject of how to be *saved* is very important. If you do not get this RIGHT, then you will miss the *game plan that God has for you to be saved*. God has written this down for us in His Word. The Bible is God's *love letter to us*. I hope you have the RIGHT BIBLE because the modern Bibles, just like the Roman Catholic Church, CHANGE the system of Salvation by Grace through Faith, to a system of Salvation by Works. Let's see how the *"Catholic promoted NIV"* deals with some verses on the doctrine of *SALVATION*.

Let's start with I Corinthians 1:18. The modern versions present SALVATION as a *PROCESS* instead of SALVATION *INSTANTANEOUSLY*.

KJB – *"For the preaching of the cross is to them that perish foolishness; but unto us which are saved it is the power of God."*

NIV – *"For the message of the cross is foolishness to those who are perishing, but to us who are being saved it is the power of God."*

I thought Ephesians 1:13 talked about the Holy Spirit, who *seals* for us the grace of God? After we look up this verse, should we not tell the scholars of the NIV that to be consistent and to show the Bible to have *no errors,* they better work on omitting Ephesians 1:13? They just lost their consistency across the Bible. The Muslims are *laughing* at us again. But I do not think that it is funny. In fact it is sad. I suppose these scholars believe in Salvation insecurity? We are in big trouble if we send out our visitation teams to witness to the Muslims with an NIV in our hands. We better take our King James Bible. It is the perfectly preserved Word of God in English.

The Roman Catholic Church also believes that you can lose your Salvation. Remember, you *cannot* get your *truth from Rome.* Do not follow the Roman Catholic system of *"works and sacraments"* to get you *saved.* If you follow the system of the Catholics, you will have *ritual, religion, and bondage.* Ritual Religion does not automatically give you a *"relationship"* with Jesus by being *"born again."* Your Salvation is *instantaneous.* Unbiblical Salvation is *progressive.* Roman Catholics carry a lot of *guilt* in their lives. Ask any Roman Catholic the two *diagnostic questions* and you will see by their answer that they have a totally different concept as to how one is to be saved. The two diagnostic questions are:

1. Have you come to the place in your spiritual life, where you know for certain, that if you were to die tonight, you would go to heaven? The only six answers that one can give are:

A. Yes

B. No

C. Maybe

D. I don't know.

E. I don't care.

F. No one can know that.

2. Let's suppose you were to die tonight, and you were to stand before God, and He were to say to you, why should I let you into my heaven, what would you say?

You will know by the answer to these questions, whether the person you are witnessing to believes Salvation by *"grace through faith,"* or if the candidate for Salvation has a *"works theology."*

As a former Roman Catholic, I never knew that I could *"know"* that I could be saved. I only had hope for *"purgatory,"* a place that does not exist. They took my money when I lit candles for the poor souls that were supposedly in purgatory. I paid the priest for *"masses,"* to be said on behalf of my dead relatives. *The Catholic Mass* crucifies the Lord again and again, in defiance of the Scriptures, as recorded in Hebrews chapters 8-10. If you are a Roman Catholic reading this, all you have to do is read these 3 chapters to see that the Bible *forbids* the sacrifice of a *Mass*.

In the Roman Catholic Church, where I spent the first 19 years of my life as an unsaved, but religious person, I had to go to AURICULAR CONFESSION every Saturday so that I could receive in a wafer the Lord Jesus Christ. This was done every week. It seemed that I *"gained grace,"* then *"I lost grace."* I would *"gain grace again,"* then *"I lost grace again."* I needed Jesus in my heart, and in my life, but they told me I could find Him in a wafer. All of their doctrines were a major distraction from a personal relationship with Jesus. There were:

Statues

Prayers to Mary

Rosary beads

Transubstantiation

Mass

Saints

The pope

Purgatory

Priests

Scapulars

Infant Baptism

But there was never the Gospel as the *Bible* preaches. I knew about Jesus, but I never received Him personally in my life through any of these things. If there are any scholars reading this, should I have to type out what I John 5:13 says in the Word of God? Does not this verse tell me and any *"saved Christian"* that they can *"know"* that they are saved? In the Roman Catholic Church, to *"know"* that you are saved, is a sin of *"presumption."* But you can't get your truth from *Rome*.

Let's look at another verse that is important to the DOCTRINE OF

SALVATION. (I Peter 2:2.)

KJB – *"As newborn babes, desire the sincere milk of the word, that ye may grow thereby."*

NIV – *"Like newborn babies, crave pure spiritual milk, so that you may grow up in your salvation."*

There are two things *"biblically wrong"* with the NIV'S rendering of this verse. First of all, the NIV omitted the *sincere milk of the Word.* Whose *"pure spiritual milk"* do they want to crave? Crave the pure spiritual milk of the *Muslims*, or *Buddha*, or the *Jehovah Witnesses*, or the *Mormons*, or the pure spiritual milk of those who preach *"another gospel,"* like the Roman Catholic Church? The NIV omits the answer to this question. We are to crave the *"pure spiritual milk of the Word."* That Word is our *final authority.* We have the "PRESERVED WORD OF GOD" in our possession. The "Judeo/Christian Bible," the "preserved word of God in English," the "KING JAMES BIBLE" is the "pure spiritual milk that all Christians should crave."

Secondly, it is unbiblical Roman Catholic theology that teaches that one has to *grow up* in their Salvation. (There are Protestant Denominations that also believe this to be biblical doctrine.) **The whore of Babylon has daughters.**

Revelation chapter 17 describes who the Bible says is the "WHORE OF BABYLON." Read this chapter and see that the Bible says you can figure this one out with wisdom, simply by identifying the five hints that the Scriptures give to you. People who are insecure in their Salvation, like the Roman Catholics and the Protestants who are apostate, have a *"do theology"* instead of a *"done theology."* (Why not check Revelation chapter 17 out right now, so that you can figure out who is the "whore" of Babylon?)

We grow up in our:

Faith

Sanctification

Good Works

Knowledge of God's Word

And in our relationship with Jesus.

But you cannot grow up in your Salvation. Salvation is in the theological category of *JUSTIFICATION* and not the theological category of *SANCTIFICATION.* If we grow up in our Salvation, then *"good works"* comes back to our justification before God, and it puts us *right where we were before we got saved.* I thought the *"impetus was on God?"* Why did we let the NIV shift the impetus of our salvation back to us?

Here is another Salvation verse changed by the NIV. Luke 9:56:

KJB – *"For the son of man is not come to destroy men's lives, but to save them. And they went to another village."*

NIV – *"And they went to another village."*

I stand corrected. This verse was not *"changed,"* it was pretty much *"omitted."* Where did this verse go? Don't you think that this verse should be in your BIBLE? Why did Westcott and Hort take this out? Why did they draw from the Manuscripts of Alexandria Egypt and the manuscripts of Siniaticus and Vaticanus, when Beza had this verse in his Greek text? The Antiochan manuscripts had this verse! The Roman Catholic Jesuits who trained Westcott and Hort trained them well from a Catholic point of view. Is the simplicity of Jesus Christ being CENTRAL TO SALVATION bothersome to the Roman Catholics?

When it comes to Salvation, *Jesus plus anything else is false.* In I Timothy 2:5 it says:

"For there is one God, and one mediator between God and men, the man Christ Jesus."

Is this too easy to UNDERSTAND? The modern Bible scholars told me that I could not UNDERSTAND the King James Bible!

I would have liked to have had the chance to *understand* Luke 9:56 and Matt. 18:11, but look what the NIV and other versions do to this verse:

KJB – *"For the son of man is come to save that which is lost."*

NIV –

NO, The printer did not forget to render the words of the NIV. What you SEE is what you GET. It is not in there. I suppose that the Greek Philosophers, the Roman Catholics, and Westcott and Hort, (Supported by the Modern Day Scholars,) forgot to put this in the NIV and other modern counterfeit versions of the Bible. Why? This verse is all about *the purpose as to why Jesus came to earth.* Once again, is Jesus being central to salvation something the aforementioned does not like?

Some will use the excuse of scribal error, but over 64,000 words are missing in the NIV! There are 5,778 verses that are different in the modern versions as compared to the King James. Even the most incompetent could not lose that many words, and besides, God promised that not one jot or tittle of His Word would pass away. Hmm! I hope your blood is boiling!

I spent a little extra time on the doctrine of salvation, because Jesus talks about *hell* in the Bible twice as much as He talks about *heaven*. He does not want us to go to hell. Salvation is important to Jesus and to us. We better get the doctrine of salvation right. I will not spend as much time on the other doctrines *attacked* by the modern Bible scholar. But each and every doctrine must be looked at, because every single one of them takes their turn omitting or changing these verses. This will affect doctrine all the time. Let's take a look at THE VIRGIN BIRTH.

The Virgin Birth

Every Christian believes in the VIRGIN BIRTH OF CHRIST. Mary, the mother of Jesus, was a virgin when she conceived. Joseph and Mary did not have any relations physically with one another until after Jesus was born. (The Roman Catholic Church makes Mary out to be a *"perpetual virgin."*) Jesus had brothers, and at least two sisters. The Roman Catholic Church lies against the Scriptures, because the Bible lists the half brothers of Jesus. (Matt. 13:55.) But look how the NIV destroys the DOCTRINE of the VIRGIN BIRTH in Luke 2:33.

KJB – *"And Joseph and his mother marveled at those things which were spoken of him."*

NIV – *"The child's father and mother marveled at what was said about him."*

Joseph was not the FATHER OF JESUS. The Holy Spirit declared Mary to be pregnant with Jesus. The HOLY GHOST is speaking in a NARRATIVE. Later, Mary calls Joseph His father in Luke 2:48, but the Lord Jesus gently corrects her in Luke 2:49. (So much for Mary being SINLESS as the Roman Catholic Church falsely preaches.) This same Mary, the earthly mother of Jesus, says that she "rejoices" in God her *"Saviour"* in Luke 1:47.

Sinless people do not need a Saviour. The "Mary" of the *Catholic church* is not the same "Mary" of the *Bible*. The Roman Catholic Church puts Mary on a pedestal equal to Christ. Yet the Bible says in Isaiah 42:8:

"I am the Lord: that is my name: and my glory will I not give to another, neither my praise to graven images."

Sin is not biologically transmitted as the Catholics would have you to believe. If that was the case then the mother of Mary would also have to be sinless. Sin is *spiritually* transmitted. Mary did not have to be *sinless* in order to be the mother of Jesus. Only God is sinless. The Catholic Church makes Mary to be SINLESS ANYWAY. The Roman Catholic doctrine of the *"immaculate conception"* did not come into history until 1854. No pope before that time made this an official doctrine of the Roman Catholic Church. It is amazing the kinds of things the human mind can make up. How many *doctrines* of the Christian faith have to be *destroyed* before you believe that there are COUNTERFEIT VERSIONS OF THE BIBLE IN YOUR MIDST? You have just been shown two, here is another example.

Let's look at the BLOOD in Colossians 1:14 and in some other verses as well.

The Doctrine of the Blood

The shed blood of Jesus Christ on the cross is absolutely essential for the remission of sin. In Hebrews 9:22 it says:

"And almost all things are by the law purged with blood; and without shedding of blood is no remission."

Watch how the NIV leaves out *"the remission of sins"* and changes this to *"leaving past sins unpunished"* in Romans 3:25.

KJB – *"Whom God hath set forth to be a propitiation through faith in his blood, to declare his righteousness for remission of sins that are past, through the forebearance of God."*

NIV – *"God presented him as a sacrifice of atonement, through faith in his blood. He did this to demonstrate His justice, because in his forbearance he had left the sins committed beforehand unpunished."*

The NIV changes *"righteousness"* to *"justice."* Justice is a weak word when compared to righteousness. *"Propitiation"* is a stronger word than *"sacrifice of atonement."* Propitiation is a word that was first found, only in the Bible. It means *"perfect sacrifice."*

More importantly, the words *"remission of sins"* should be in the text, because it doesn't just say he had left the sins committed beforehand unpunished. It says the sins were remitted. Remitted is clear as to what the blood does. It remits our sin, so as to remove it *completely*. The preserved manuscripts and Greek text have *"remission of sins."*

It is true that the NIV does not completely take out the BLOOD of CHRIST. But it weakens it to a lower level by choosing different words than what God chose. Let's look at Rev. 1:5b as an example.

NIV – *"To him who loves us and has freed us from our sins by his blood."*

KJB – *"Unto him that loved us, and washed us from our sins in his own blood."*

Not only is *"washed"* stronger than *"freed"* but bad *"theology"* comes about by omitting the word OWN from BLOOD.

Some theologians conclude that it was not Jesus' physical blood that saves us, but just His dying on our behalf, which is symbolized by the shedding of His physical blood. The Bible tells us otherwise. If the Blood does not save, then we have to take out the following verses: Romans 5:9, Eph. 1:7, Eph. 2:13, Col. 1:20, and Heb. 9:12.

These theologians conclude that Jesus had Human Blood and that in the *"blood itself,"* sin can not be cleansed. *The saving just comes from the cross.* Well, saving does come from the cross, but because the blood was shed. In Leviticus 17:11 it says:

"For it is the blood that maketh an atonement for the soul."

Jesus had *"God's blood"* according to I Tim. 3:16. Jesus was *"God manifest in the flesh."* He had God's blood!

In I John 1:7, the NIV uses the word purify instead of CLEANSETH. CHRIST IS ALSO LEFT OUT IN THIS VERSE. Jesus Christ does more than just purify. HE CLEANS SIN UP COMPLETELY, He doesn't just MAKE IT BETTER.

The strongest case against the NIV concerning the BLOOD is found in Col. 1:14. Look at what is taken out of this verse.

KJB – *"In whom we have redemption through his blood, even the forgiveness of sins."*

NIV – *"In whom we have redemption, the forgiveness of sins."*

Where is the blood in this verse? Why was it taken out? What spirit wants to take this doctrine down a notch in the newer versions like the NIV? Could it be the same spirit that makes *Jesus*:

Fall?

Sin?

Come from an unruly genealogy?

Jesus coming in the place of the *enemy*?

No standard against the enemy?

Confuse the Mark of the Beast?

Change Salvation from *"grace through faith"* to Salvation by *"works?"*

Make Joseph to be Jesus' father?

Dilute the blood from redemption?

HMMM! I hope you can see that something is wrong with this picture.

The NIV scholars apparently believe that there is NO POWER IN THE BLOOD. I suppose we should take out the hymn, "POWER IN THE BLOOD." The modern version churches should not sing this hymn any longer. Chances are that many of them have already stopped singing that there is *"POWER IN THE BLOOD."* While Christian music is not God breathed, the hymn says that there is *"WONDER WORKING POWER IN THE BLOOD."* Jesus, being God in the flesh, had GOD'S BLOOD. The *blood* shed on the *cross* redeems us, because *"only"* the *BLOOD OF GOD HIMSELF* can cleanse away our sin. Why would the NIV scholars want to dilute the Blood of Jesus in these verses?

The Godhead

The main doctrine that separates us from the Jehovah Witnesses is the *"doctrine of the Godhead."* Not only do the Jehovah Witnesses confuse this doctrine by telling others that Jesus is "just the son of God," but also the Roman Catholic Church has brought much confusion to the simple point that *"Jesus is God."*

The Roman Catholic Church uses "unbiblical" terms like *"TRINITY AND PERSONS."* The Bible uses the terms *"GODHEAD AND MANIFESTATIONS."* The Jehovah Witnesses deny altogether that JESUS IS GOD. Rome would have you believe that the GODHEAD is about 3 different *"PERSONS OR ENTITIES."* They may not believe in three separate Gods, but they bring confusion to this simple doctrine by using the words *"trinity,"* and *"persons,"* in their explanation of the *"Godhead."* The Bible teaches us that there is *"ONE GOD, WHO MANIFESTS HIMSELF THREE WAYS"* as *Father, Son, and Holy Spirit.* The Bible emphasizes that there is just *ONE* God. You should not use words that might suggest that there is more than *one* God.

Simply put, all we have to know to understand this doctrine is that *"JESUS IS GOD."* In John 1:1 it says:

"In the beginning was the Word. The Word was with God. And the Word was God."

In John 10:30 it says:

"I and my Father are one."

The strongest verse on the GODHEAD is found in I John 5:7-8. Watch how tricky the NIV is in disguising the fact that they totally remove several words.

Let's look at how they virtually drop the end of verse 7, but put the number 7 in the Bible so that it looks like no verse is missing. They then drop part of verse 8. You might also notice that the NIV puts their numbers in the middle of the paragraph instead of down the side of the Bible. They do this so that you cannot easily detect that they have removed a whole verse. Let's compare.

KJB – *"For there are three that bear record in heaven, the Father, the Word, and Holy Ghost: And these three are one. And there are three that bear witness in earth, the Spirit, and the water, and the blood: And these three agree in one."*

NIV - *"For there are three that testify. The Spirit, the water and the blood: And the three are in agreement."*

In the NIV'S verse 7, the scholars don't even make the testimony to be in HEAVEN. *HEAVEN IS OMITTED. THE FATHER, THE WORD, AND THE HOLY GHOST ARE OMITTED ALSO.* Notice that in the NIV'S verse 8, the three are in agreement as if they are *SEPARATE ENTITIES.*

The KJB simply says that these three, *WHO ARE ONE, AGREE IN ONE.* I wonder how many Jehovah Witnesses have been won by NIV visitation teams. Why would they take a *"dull sword"* with them, when they could take a *"sharp sword"* with them by using the preserved Word of God in English, the King James Bible?

The King James Bible is the Bible that the *DEVIL LOVES TO HATE AND THE BIBLE THAT THE ROMAN CATHOLIC CHURCH TRIED TO DESTROY.* (Check your history concerning the "Gun powder plot" during the reign of King James.) Satan does not rest. He is alive and well in the age of Laodicea using modern Bible scholarship to attack the Word of God.

Satan's so-called *"scholars"* put out a new Bible at least once a year. When you compare these *"new Bibles"* with the *"preserved Word of God,"* the *doctrines* continue to change for the worse, a little at a time, in the newer versions. All you have to do is compare the more recent ones, like the *"Message"* with the NIV and the *"New World Translation,"* the latter of which is the Bible of the Jehovah Witnesses.

Repentance

It is true that the NIV does not remove the word REPENTANCE in all of its verses. (But the *"New King James,"* changes the word *"repentance"* to the word *"relent"* 44 times. The strategy of the modern-day scholar is to remove a little at a time. If the NIV translators removed the word *REPENTANCE IN EVERY VERSE, THEY WOULD SHOW THEMSELVES TO BE A FRAUD.* It remains to be seen what they will do when their *"new revisions"* are out. They intend to update their Bible every 10 years or so.

They have already come out with the *"TNIV"* That stands for *"Today's New International Version."* It is *"different,"* and yes, *"it is worse."* They want to be *"politically correct,"* and neutralize *"men."* They will then proceed to *"neutralize God."* Watch for the newer versions on the market to eventually make these changes.

This is the direction that they are taking the people that trust and follow them. This neutralizing of man and eventually God, is being done in the *"New King James Version"* as well. The Bible tells us that there is nothing *"new"* under the sun. The "new" King James version is the *"King Agrippa of Bible versions."* It *almost* has it right. Therefore it is one of the most dangerous versions out there because it seems to some that it is the perfect compromise between the NIV and the preserved Word of God. This is far from the truth. The *"new"* King James has many problems in it as well. A tract written by Dr. Sam Gipp on the *"New King James"* states that the *"New King James"* deletes the following:

"Lord" 66 times.

"Jehovah" entirely.

"blood" 23 times.

"damnation" entirely.

"fornication" 23 times.

"heaven" 50 times.

"God" 51 times.

"repent" 44 times.

"hell" 22 times.

"soul" 137 times.

"devil" 26 times.

"New Testament" entirely.

The NIV Translation Committee believes that language changes all the time. Where this may be true concerning *"language,"* we know that this does not affect God, because He *NEVER CHANGES.* HE GETS IT RIGHT THE FIRST TIME. This claim that language is always changing is merely an excuse for the NIV translators to put out a new Bible every couple of years or so, and make more money. Furthermore, they encourage *"women and homosexuals"* to be in the pulpit.

With every *"new Bible"* we can expect that something else will be omitted, and some other doctrine will be changed. Yet, the Bible tells us in the book of Ecclesiastes that there is nothing *"new under the sun."* We shall watch and see as time and history will prove this to be right.

Now, watch and see with your own eyes what the NIV does to *DELETE* the subject of *REPENTANCE*. It takes this doctrine down a notch in two GOSPEL VERSES. (Some people only read the GOSPELS.) Let's look at Matt. 9:13 and Mark 2:17:

NIV – *"But go and learn what this means: I desire mercy, not sacrifice. For I have not come to call the righteous, but sinners."*

KJB – *"But go ye and learn what that meaneth. I will have mercy, and not sacrifice: For I am not come to call the righteous, but sinners to repentance."*

To what is the NIV calling the sinners to come? Is the NIV calling the sinners to the dinner table? God's preserved Word is clear. He is calling the *"sinners"* to *"repentance."* We have a *"manuscript"* for this verse so why is it not used?

This verse is partially repeated in Mark 2:17 with the same result. Both verses have Jesus saying that he calls the *"sinners to repent."* The NIV removes repentance in both of these Gospel verses. What Spirit in the NIV wants Jesus to:

Fall?

Sin?

Come from an unruly genealogy?

Come in place of the enemy?

Have no standard against that enemy?

Confuse the Mark of the Beast?

Make Salvation into Works?

Deny the Virgin Birth?

Dilute the Blood?

Delete repentance from two Gospel verses?

Could it be the same Spirit that does not want to call homosexuality a sin?

Homosexuality

It is politically incorrect to believe that homosexuality is sin. If homosexuality is not sin, then God must apologize to Sodom and Gomorrah. Homosexuals take the position that their situation is *"hereditary."* Homosexuals believe that the way they choose to be cannot be helped. They believe that they were born homosexual. This indicts God concerning his consistency in the way He created us.

It is true that the Bible tells us to *love* all sinners. However, we are to love the *"sinner"* and *"hate all sin."* The Bible tells us that homosexuality is sin. This is listed in the books of Leviticus, Romans, I Corinthians, and II Timothy among other books of the Bible.

Since we are Bible believing Christians, we cannot agree with their position. Yet, at the same time, we have *no ax to grind* against any *individual* homosexual. Our prayers are that the homosexual and lesbian individual would be saved, and *recant* their position. Christians should pray that they will change their heart toward this belief, and live a lifestyle that is pleasing to God.

Many Christian ministries have helped homosexuals to be free from this bondage. They re-learned how to have a biblical perspective on God's plan for a man and a woman in the bond of *"marriage."* Biblical *marriage*, and the biblical *concepts of family,* as God planned it to be, are under severe attack. Today, more then ever, *people live together in sin.*

The modern Bibles, like the NIV and others, go soft on the Christian position that is laid out for us in the *"preserved Word of God"* in English, the King James Bible. Virginia Mollencott was on the Committee of Bible Translators for the NIV. She was influential in making changes in the NIV that favor the view of how homosexuals feel about themselves. Here is what has been changed, and the significance of the changes. Let's look at Romans 1:28.

KJB – *"And even as they did not like to retain God in their knowledge, God gave them over to a reprobate mind, to do those things which are not convenient."*

NIV – *"Furthermore, since they did not think it worthwhile to retain the knowledge of God, he gave them over to a depraved mind to do what ought not to be done."*

You might be saying that this is picky. What is the problem? Well, we all are *depraved.* But we are not all *reprobate.* Homosexuality is now a sin, like any other sin. It is true that *all* sin separates us from God, and there is *no degree* to any sin that is not forgiven when it comes to being saved. But the consequences of some sin, like homosexuality, are definitely more graven. The graveness of the sin of homosexuality is taken out of the Bible by the NIV.

Let's look at another example of the "water down," from II Timothy 3:3.

KJB – "*Without natural affection, trucebreakers, false accusers, incontinent, fierce, despisers of those that are good.*"

NIV – "*Without love, unforgiving, slanderous, without self-control, brutal, not lovers of the good.*"

The NIV changes "*without natural affection*" to "*without love.*" Without natural affection is clearly talking about those who do not naturally follow God's laws concerning sex. This includes homosexuality. We know that God created male and female. By changing "*without natural affection*" to "*without love*" the NIV not only protects the homosexual, it indicts anyone who might call their sin to be sin, as an unloving person who hates. Even though the Bible clearly says that homosexuality is sin. The case can be made that it would be unlovely to say that homosexuality is a sin. Virginia Mollencott knew how to effectively make a *play on words.*

Let's look at the most dangerous change that was made by this committee. Look at I Corinthians 6:9. Beware of the law of the "*hate crime.*" For Christians will someday be sent to jail for what they "*say*" instead of what they "*do.*"

KJB – "*Know ye not that the unrighteous shall not inherit the kingdom of God? Be not deceived: neither fornicators, nor idolaters, nor adulterers, nor effeminate, nor abusers of themselves with mankind.*"

NIV – "*Do you not know that the wicked will not inherit the kingdom of God? Do not be deceived: neither the sexually immoral, nor idolaters, nor adulterers, nor male prostitutes, nor homosexual offenders.*"

The NIV changes "*abusers of themselves with mankind*" to "*homosexual offenders.*" It can now be interpreted that anyone who "*offends*" a "*homosexual*" will not "*inherit the kingdom of God.*" "*Abusers of themselves with mankind*" is clear. This is about homosexuals and lesbians. These words are about all kinds of perverted sex, including homosexuality.

This story is true. A homosexual went into a pastor's office one day and asked him if he felt that homosexuality was a *sin.* The pastor replied that he believed that God himself makes this clear in His Word and that it is a sin. The homosexual had an NIV in his hand and told the pastor that he was the one who was sinning and that he was the one who was going to hell. He read the NIV verse to him and said that since he was a "*homosexual*" he was "*offended*" by the pastor. The homosexual proclaimed that the pastor who offended him was not going to inherit the kingdom of God. He said, "See, right here in your Bible it says, *'homosexual offenders.'*" He left the office feeling victory in his heart. The pastor never had a chance to tell him that the Bible he was using was a COUNTERFEIT.

In the following verses, the word "sodomite," is substituted for the words *"male shrine prostitute"* in most of the post 1881 Bible versions that draw their text from Westcott and Hort, and other so-called scholars like Nestle and Aland. Here is a list of those verses.

Deut. 23:17

I Kings 14:24

I Kings 15:12

I Kings 22:46

II Kings 23:7

Remember there will be no repentance/revival until our pastors preach the truth about the changing of the preserved Word of God in English, the King James Bible. All the average Christian has to do is compare these verses himself. The lie that has been told about understanding and readability is false. Doctrine and Theology have been changed. You will not hear this from most pastors. These men have done you a disservice by not addressing this subject. You are going to have to do your own investigation. As you pray for revival, remember to measure the cost. This will definitely upset your *"comfort zones."*

Worship

How come the NIV does not like to worship Jesus? We, as Christians, worship Jesus because Jesus is God and is deserving of all our worship and praise. The preserved Word of God records people in the Bible who worshipped Jesus, because of who Jesus claimed to be, and because of the miracles that He performed.

Look at what the NIV does to the doctrine of "worship." Let's look at Matthew 9:18 and Matthew 8:2:

KJB – *"While he spake these things unto them, behold, there came a certain ruler, and worshipped him saying, My daughter is even now dead: but come and lay thy hand upon her, and she shall live."*

NIV – *"While he was saying this, a ruler came and knelt before him and said, "My daughter has just died. But come and put your hand on her, and she will live."*

You can kneel and not worship. You can be kneeling because of feeling down trodden or burdened. A baseball player kneels in the *"on deck circle."* I doubt he is worshipping God. He might be praying for a hit, but he can pray in the dugout too. Kneeling is not always significant to worship. We can worship God in our heart while we are walking our dog. The KJB is clear. The ruler worshipped Jesus because Jesus was worthy of being worshipped. The NIV just has the ruler kneeling but does not mention *"worship."* In another healing situation, a leper *worships* Jesus when he asks for a healing. Let's look at Matthew 8:2:

KJB – *"And, behold, there came a leper and worshipped him, saying, Lord, if thou wilt, thou canst make me clean."*

NIV – *"A man with leprosy came and knelt before him and said, Lord, if you are willing, you can make me clean."*

Once again the NIV implies that when one kneels, one is *worshipping*. A carpenter kneels sometimes when he is working. A sport figure can kneel when he is hurt. Kneeling is not symbolic to worship. We can worship Jesus in our heart and with our lips without kneeling. The arms of the heart of the leper were wide open. He was worshipping Jesus. Jesus saw his heart. He may or may not have been kneeling.

The Bible makes it clear that worship has nothing to do with *"when"* or *"where"* we worship. God is not interested in our rituals and habits. The woman at the well in John chapter four found out that according to Jesus, we were to worship God in *Spirit and Truth*. This is recorded in John 4:23. God looks into our heart. He is not interested in the time and place that we worship, or whether or not we are kneeling.

The word *worship* was purposely taken out of the text in Matt. 9:18 and in Matt. 8:2. Why would the NIV *"worship"* a Jesus that they make to:

Fall?

Sin?

Come from an unruly genealogy?

Come in place of the enemy?

Have no standard against the enemy?

Confuse the Mark of the Beast?

Make Salvation into works?

Deny the virgin birth?

Dilute the blood?

Delete repentance?

Water down homosexuality?

De-emphasize worship?

The answer to this question is that while they do all these things, they certainly would not use the word worship when it comes to Jesus. How come?

Chick Saliby tells us in his book, *If the Foundations be Destroyed* (page 26) that the Greek word for worship is *"proskuneo."* Saliby goes on to comment that the NIV does not translate the word "proskuneo" when it comes to Jesus, but the NIV goes ahead and uses the word for worship when it comes to:

A servant (Rev. 19:10)

An angel (Rev. 22:8)

False religion (John 4:20,22)

Idols (Acts 7:43)

The image of the beast (Rev. 13:15, 16:2, 19:20)

The beast (Rev. 13:4, 8, 12)

The beast and the image (Rev. 14:9, 11; 20:4)

Demons and idols (Rev. 9:20)

The dragon (Satan) (Rev. 13:4)[18]

Why didn't the NIV use *"proskuneo,"* when it came to worshipping Jesus?

Mary, a Perpetual Virgin?

The Roman Catholic Church deceives their indoctrinated parishioners into believing that Mary did not have any relations with Joseph after Jesus was born. Therefore, they contend that Jesus did not have any brothers or sisters. They believe, *without scriptural proof,* that Mary was a *"perpetual virgin."* This is another lie, and another false doctrine. Once again, the false doctrines of Rome, uninspired by the Holy Spirit, (the true vicar of Christ) do not line up with the Scriptures.

The Scriptures are clear. Jesus had half brothers and sisters, as recorded in the Gospel of Matthew and Mark, and in I Corinthians and the book of Galatians. The brothers are named, but the sisters are not named. However, we know that there are at least two sisters. Let's go to the *"true church fathers"* the writers of the Bible. Rome has its own set of *church fathers.*

Matthew 13:55-56:

---

18. Salliby, Chick. *If the Foundations Be Destroyed.* (Word and Prayer Ministries: Fiskdale, MA, 1973) p. 26.

"Is not this the carpenter's son? Is not his mother called Mary? And his brethren, James, and Joses, and Simon, and Judas? And his sisters, are they not all with us? Whence then hath this man all these things?"

Mark 6:3 says:

"Is not this the carpenter, the son of Mary, the brother of James, and Joses, and of Judah, and Simon? And are not his sisters here with us? And they were offended at him."

I Corinthians 9:5 says:

"Have we not power to lead about a sister, a wife, as well as other apostles, and as the brethren of the Lord, and Cephas?"

Galatians 1:19 says:

"But other of the Apostles saw I none, save James the Lord's brother."

Look at what the NIV and the other modern versions of the Bible do to protect this false Roman Catholic doctrine. In Matt.1:25 the NIV takes out the word "firstborn." Let's compare.

KJB – "And knew her not till she had brought forth her firstborn son: and he called his name Jesus."

NIV – "But he had no union with her until she gave birth to a son. And he gave him the name Jesus."

This verse puts the NIV another step closer to the Catholic doctrine that Mary is a perpetual virgin. They left the word *until* in the text, but they took the word *firstborn* out of the text. Don't forget that Cardinal Martini, of the Catholic Church, was on the committee of Bible translators for the NIV. Why Cardinal Martini and Virginia Mollencott were on this committee is beyond me. But they were both instrumental in passing their own agendas and placing them in the Scriptures without the flock knowing. That sounds like the Democratic Party.

Prayer and Fasting

Prayer and fasting are two powerful disciplines that are available to all Christians. Many Christians pray but few utilize fasting as something they would do in every day life. We usually *"fast"* to enter into a tough spiritual battle. You do not hear too much preaching on the subject of *"fasting."* Are the Christians of Laodicea as disciplined enough spiritually to utilize fasting, as much as Christians who lived in another age of church history? I bet you they fasted in the past, more than we do in the age that we live. When was the last time you heard your pastor preach on the subject of fasting? Honestly, when was the last time that you have fasted for something? What can *"prayer and fasting"* do for us that one without the other cannot do?

Let's go back to another comparison verse on this important doctrine. We will go to Matt. 17:21:

KJB – *"Howbeit this kind goeth not out but by prayer and fasting."*

NIV –

Once again, this is not a misprint. There is no verse rendered here by the NIV except in the footnotes. If you read this verse in the context of the chapter, you will see that Jesus is telling His disciples that certain devils cannot be cast out, unless the believer *prays and fasts.* Only with *"fasting"* added to *"prayer"* will the devil leave a person who is possessed. This is not an ordinary spiritual battle. Not every Christian is qualified to battle with those spirits who possess the soul of some who have opened themselves up to be possessed. These possessed people are not only unsaved, they have dabbled into higher realms of spirituality that go beyond the norm.

The disciples wanted Jesus to tell them why they could not cast out the devil from a boy whose father was concerned over his son, as his son kept falling into the fire and into the water. The boy's own father called him a lunatic. Jesus gave to His disciples, and to us, the spiritual secret of dealing with such people. The NIV does not have this powerful verse on the doctrine of *"prayer and fasting."* They put this verse in the footnotes, but they do not put this verse in the text. This verse does not belong in the footnotes. *This verse belongs in the text.*

The only reason they put this verse in the footnotes is because they have been taken to task by the honest scholar who keeps this verse in the text where it belongs. We have a manuscript for this verse. The modern day scholar knows that we have a manuscript for this verse, so he deceivingly puts it in the footnotes. Once again, be honest, how many of us read those footnotes? About as many of us who *fast.* Not too many! Without this verse readily available in the text, the preacher reading his Bible simply does not have this verse to even know that a special spiritual battle must be fought in this way. Since the people do not hear too much preaching on prayer and fasting, most people rarely ever battle the devil in this area, because we simply are not equipped to do so. Neither are we reminded by our pastor, that fasting along with prayer is possible.

Chapter Six

More Doctrinal Problems in the NIV– Christ's Omnipresence

God has attributes that man can never have, and can never fully understand. God is *omnipotent*. That is to say, *He is all powerful.* He holds the universe together. He sends and stops the rain. Thunder and lightning remind us of the power of God. Dare we not respect His power? He controls our next breath. All life and death is in His hands.

Wouldn't it be nice to get a chance to golf against a perfect God, who is not only *perfect*, but who is also *"all powerful?"* I wonder to myself if it would be boring or exciting to watch perfection step up to the tee. I suppose it would be both boring and exciting. It would be *boring*, in that the outcome of the game would be automatic. *He will golf a perfect game.* A hole in one every time he hits from the tee. He needs only the club that drives the ball. But it sure would be *exciting* watching Him get there. God would have to call His shot, so that no one can say He was lucky. I sense He would get quite creative. How about a shot from the tee, using a putter, that ricochets off several trees, then drops in the hole without it grazing the flag stick? What if it hit the top of the flag stick, and literally passes through the top of the stick down into the hole? It has never been done. God can do it.

God is also *omniscient*. That is to say that He is "all knowing." He knows our every thought. I think it would be scary to be a mind reader. In our human nature, we would overreact when the thoughts of others do not turn out to be favorable. God handles our thoughts very well. He does not overreact. The Bible says in Jeremiah 1:5 that God knew us before we were formed.

"Before I formed thee in the belly I knew thee; and before thou camest forth out of the womb I sanctified thee, and I ordained thee a prophet unto the nations."

Every abortionist should read this verse. The abortionist claims that abortion is not murder, because the baby has not yet come out of the belly. The baby is just a *"fetus"* and not a person. Yet, God knew who we were before we were born.

God is also omnipresent. That is to say that *"He is everywhere."* While Jesus was in Mary's womb, He was still holding up the universe. The moon did not crash into the sun.

Gravity still held all the people on earth and kept them from floating out into space. Whether He was in heaven or being born on earth to a virgin, He was still God. His presence in the womb did not change anything that He made with His power.

In John 3:13 the Bible shows us that the Lord's Divine ability to be everywhere at once was not interrupted while He lived His life on earth. Here is what the verse says:

KJB – *"And no man hath ascended up to heaven, but he that came down from heaven, even the Son of man which is in heaven."*

NIV - *"No one has ever gone into heaven except the one who came from heaven-the Son of man."*

Why were these vital words removed? This verse lays evidence to the Deity of Christ. He remained God while He was every bit a man on earth. This verse destroys Christ's *omnipresence*. No other verse in the Bible points to His *omnipresence* like this verse. Why was this verse targeted? Why is there a consistent de-emphasis on all that Jesus Christ was and is, in the Scriptures? What do the modern versions have against Jesus? Why do they go out of their way to bring Jesus down whenever they can conveniently get this by our pastor and ultimately passed us?

What scholar does not want to recognize that Jesus Christ was unique in being God? Is it the same spirit that shows Jesus to:

Fall in His own Bible?

Sin?

Come from an unruly genealogy?

Have no standard for the enemy?

Confuse the Mark of the Beast?

Make Salvation into works?

Deny the virgin birth?

Dilute the blood?

Delete repentance?

Excuse homosexuality as a serious sin?

De-emphasize worship?

Promote Catholic doctrines?

Diffuse the power of prayer and fasting?

Diminish Christ's omnipresence?

I smell a conspiracy of the devil. There is shame on all the pastors for not revealing this information to us, and for allowing the scholars to change the doctrines of the Christian belief. The Jesuits did a good job on our scholars. We should not let them get away with this tragedy. We, the people, must stand up for the truth and expose these counterfeit versions of the Bible.

Miracles

Only God can perform miracles. It is a miracle every time we take our next breath. The heart keeps pumping blood into our entire system every second. Do you know that if your heartbeat is off of its timing, it can actually make your wrist watch to slow down? It is a miracle how the eye is so connected to the brain that we can see the world in pictures. Those who are blind or who have impaired vision can tell you how fortunate you are to have all the parts of your body functioning as normal.

The Bible teaches us in many different parts of Scripture that Jesus performed many miracles such as:

Healing the blind.

Making the lame to walk.

Changing water into wine.

Walking on water.

Removing devils from the possessed.

Raising the dead.

Among many other recorded and non-recorded miracles.

Since Jesus was God, He was able to perform miracles. The people who argue that Jesus was not God would like to also argue that He did not perform any miracles either. However, we who are Christians, believe in the miracles of Jesus. The NIV and other modern versions of the Bible apparently do not believe in the miracles of God when it comes to John 5:4. Let's compare this verse in the NIV and in the preserved Word of God in English.

KJB – *"For an angel went down at a certain season into the pool, and troubled the water: whosoever then first after the troubling of the water stepped in was made whole of whatsoever disease he had."*

NIV –

Sorry, someone on the committee of Bible translators in the NIV did not want to put this verse in the text where it belongs. Please make note of this and be sure to ask your pastor on Sunday morning what he thinks about this omission. Don't let him give you any other answer except that he just didn't realize what the so-called scholars took out of the Bible. Anything else he renders would be a quick justification for preaching in a counterfeit.

Although the NIV records other miracles of Jesus, it has no excuse for taking this specific miracle of God out of the Bible. If the devil is given an inch, he will take much more than a mile. Every doctrine that the Bible teaches us should be protected and preserved in the Word of God. Don't let any scholar or pastor take the doctrines of our faith down a single notch. Challenge them in every place of the Bible that these scholars have changed the Word of God.

The Incarnation

God took on the biological process of becoming a man by entering the womb of Mary, His earthly mother. He was 100% man and 100% God. This doctrine is called the *"deity of Christ."* The incarnation deals with the *man* part of His Deity. Watch what the NIV does to de-emphasize this doctrine. Please look up Eph. 5:30. Note what the NIV removes from this verse.

NIV – *"For we are members of his body."*

KJB – *"For we are members of his body, of his flesh, and of his bones."*

Why did the NIV take these words out? There is no other explanation except that everything to do with any doctrine that concerns Jesus, the NIV either *changes*, *deletes*, or chooses not to *emphasize the doctrine*. What does the NIV have against Jesus?

The Only Requirement for Baptism

The Roman Catholic Church baptizes infants. They claim that this is necessary for Salvation. Infant baptism qualifies the Catholic to receive the rest of their sacraments. If baptism is necessary for Salvation, then Jesus would not have had to go to the cross and shed His *own* blood to save us. All He would have had to do was immerse us in water. Any person, who gets baptized without knowing Jesus as his Saviour, has become a *wet sinner* as opposed to a *dry sinner*. That is all that he has gained without Christ in his heart. No water can ever take the place of the *"blood of Christ."*

The Bible gives us one requirement for baptism. That requirement is *belief*. All believers in Christ should be baptized, because it is in *obedience* to Christ that we would be responding to His command to do so. However, the thief on the cross did not have time to be baptized. He simply believed on the Lord Jesus. He was saved without baptism. Baptism does not save us in itself. We get baptized *because* we are saved. We do not get baptized to *get* saved. Jesus said that the thief on the cross would be in paradise with him that very same day.

When the act of baptism is done, the faith of the person getting baptized is increased. The people who are watching the baptism are also encouraged in their faith. They get to see the person getting baptized give a public profession of their faith. It is a win/win situation for every one concerned.

The Catholic promoted NIV would like to change that. They omit an important verse in Acts 8:37. The *one* requirement for baptism is stated in this verse. Take a look at this and see how the Catholic promoted NIV supports the false doctrine of infant baptism. This verse addresses all forms of *"baptismal regeneration."* Baptismal regeneration is a *heresy*.

In verse 36 of Acts chapter 8, the eunuch asked Philip what was hindering him to be baptized. They were near the water so this was a timely question for the eunuch to ask this question. Philip replies in verse 37:

KJB – *"And Philip said, if thou believest with all thine heart, thou mayest. And he answered and said, I believe that Jesus Christ is the Son of God."*

NIV –

The NIV completely omits this verse from the text. Remember, Cardinal Carlo Martini, a Roman Catholic Jesuit, was on the committee of the NIV. He was instrumental in making sure that this verse was omitted from this verse. The NIV was supposed to be a Protestant Bible. Who in Protestantism is holding hands with Rome? Have the Protestants lost their protest against the false doctrines of Rome? Strange bedfellows!

Note: There are Protestant denominations who believe in "infant baptism," as an essential means to Salvation. It is "essential" to obedience but not unto Salvation. If it were essential to Salvation, then it would be a "work" and the "impetus" of getting saved would be on us to do something for ourselves. The thief on the cross would miss out, because he didn't have time to get "baptized." This corrupted doctrine was given to us by Rome. The Bible refutes this false doctrine.

Christ the Creator

We have already seen that the NIV and the other modern Bible versions show doubt when it comes to showing the *omnipresence* of Jesus, and in the *Godhead* as well. So it should not be any surprise, that when it comes to the Scriptures pointing to Jesus as the *"creator,"* that the NIV will omit important words that prove Jesus to be *"Christ the creator."* Let's compare Ephesians 3:9 in the NIV and in the KJB.

NIV – *"And to make plain to everyone the administration of this mystery, which for ages past was kept hidden in God, who created all things."*

KJB – *"And to make all men see what is the fellowship of the mystery, which from the beginning of the world hath been hid in God, who created all things by Christ Jesus."*

Jesus Christ is God. God created the world. Therefore Jesus created the world. God and Jesus are *one and the same.* God is the one who died for our sins. You don't think He would create another being other then Himself to suffer on the cross in His place, do you? If Jesus is not God, there is no sacrifice for our sins. You cannot purposely leave Jesus out of a verse concerning the subject of Creation. Jesus was there from the beginning *as God.*

The NIV leaves Jesus out of this verse in Eph. 3:9, and when it comes to certain titles referring to Jesus, the NIV strikes again by leaving:

Jesus.

Christ.

Lord.

Out of the verse. Let's take a look at some titles of our Saviour.

Title Lord

(I Cor. 15:47)

NIV – "*The first man was of the dust of the earth, the second man from heaven.*"

KJB – "*The first man is of the earth, earthy: the second man is the Lord from heaven.*"

Title Christ

(II John 9)

NIV – "*Anyone who runs ahead and does not continue in the teaching of Christ does not have God: whoever continues in the teaching has both the Father and the Son.*"

KJB – "*Whosoever transgresseth, and abideth not in the doctrine of Christ, hath not God. He that abideth in the doctrine of Christ, He hath both the Father and the Son.*"

Title Jesus

(Matt. 16:20)

NIV – "*Then he warned his disciples not to tell anyone that he was the Christ.*"

KJB – "*Then he charged his disciples that they should tell no man, that he was Jesus the Christ.*"

Some other examples of the *titles* of Jesus missing in Scripture are found in the following verses to name just a few:

John 4:42

Acts 20:21

Romans 1:3

One more side note that is very interesting concerning the NIV, and the spirit that the NIV projects. Whenever the NIV spells the word Saviour, it only uses six letters. Six is the number of man; seven is the number of God. The KJB renders, Saviour. The NIV renders Savior. Savi*our*... Is not Jesus *our* Saviour?

See just a few examples of this.

Titus 2:10

Titus 2:13

Titus 3:4

Titus 3:6

Some argue that's just the difference between America and Britain. For example, the British spell color as colour. Behavior as behaviour.

Well, if it were only a matter of American spelling, then the modern British Bibles would spell it "saviour." But, the English Standard Version, which is another counterfeit Bible, spells it Savior, too! It's not just "American" spelling. It is about the fact that they want to change the Scripture. That makes it wrong.

Christ's Eternal Existence

Jesus was always in existence from the beginning. He was not a created being who came into existence for the first time in Mary's womb. As we said before, *Jesus was God in the flesh.* This verse is found in I Tim. 3:16.

The prophet Micah told about Jesus being born in Micah 5:2. He testifies to the fact that Jesus was from the beginning. The NIV does no such thing.

NIV – *"But you, Bethlehem Ephrathah, though you are small among the clans of Judah, out of you will come for me one who will be ruler over Israel, whose origins are from of old, from ancient times."*

KJB – *"But thou Bethlehem Ephratah, though thou be little among the thousands of Judah, yet out of thee shall he come forth unto me that is to be ruler in Israel; whose goings forth have been from of old, from everlasting."*

In the NIV, Jesus is just a very old man from ancient times who was prophesied about. The preserved Word of God clarifies just how old Jesus was in existence. He was from *"everlasting."* Jesus had *no beginning.* The NIV even misspells Ephratah.

Hell

I was in a conversation with an atheist one day who said that he did not believe in the existence of God. He also does not believe in the truth of the Bible. Therefore, he does not believe that there is a place in the Bible that is called HELL. My answer to him was that he does not have to *believe* in hell to go there. His belief in the existence of hell is not a *"requirement."* A life void of God, will realize the reality of "hell" soon enough, whether the person believes it exist or believes it does not exist. If we trust in everything that man believes as opposed to what God says, we are taking a lot of chances in life that defy the percentages of *danger*. This is called *"stupidity."*

How dare we call God a liar? God, not only knows that He created a place for all those who *choose* to reject him. He also knows that it is His choice that we choose *not* to go to HELL. God desires that we choose HEAVEN. He talks about HELL, twice as much as He speaks about HEAVEN in the Scriptures, because He does not want us to go to HELL. But He cannot make that choice for us. He will not interfere in our *"free will."* He will allow us to be *stupid*. It is our choice.

Hell is a real place. The Bible is *specific* and *vivid* in its description of "hell." Someone else once told me that they don't mind going to hell, because all their friends are going to be there. This person made that statement without reading the Bible. That was a bad move. I would rather *believe* in hell and be *wrong*, than say there is no hell and come to find out that God was *right* all along. That would be another move that comes from *stupidity*.

There is no friendship in HELL. *You are on your own.* There will be *"wailing"* and *"gnashing"* of teeth. That is made clear in Matt. 8:12. If that is friendship, then it is going to be my friends against your friends, and we are both going to get *punched* in the *mouth*. Put your boxing gloves on your hands. There is going to be a *rumble*.

If HELL is a real place (and it is), then the subject of hell is not a *laughing* matter. It should not be taken *lightly*. If the Scriptures given by God are *"vivid"* and *"specific,"* how dare we change the Scriptures in any way? But you guessed it right, that is exactly what the NIV has done. The description of hell in the NIV is much less *"horrible"* than the description God gives to us in His Word.

Let us once again compare, so we can see this with our own eyes and not be blind as Revelation describes us to be. Look up Rev. 20:1.

NIV - *"And I saw an angel coming down out of heaven, having the key to the Abyss and holding in his hand a great chain."*

KJB – *"And I saw an angel come down from heaven, having the key of the bottomless pit and a great chain in his hand."*

What is the *Abyss*, a nice easy wonderland? I thought the NIV rendered easier words for us to understand? I'm glad the Word of God defines what the Abyss is supposed to be. It is a *"bottomless pit."* Now I can know that wherever hell is, I am going to get further and further away from God as time goes on. *There is no end to my falling away from God.* Got your parachute?

Let's take a look at some more verses. Look at Psalm 11:6:

NIV – *"On the wicked he will rain fiery coals and burning sulfur: a scorching wind will be their lot."*

So far my picture of hell in this verse is that the possibility of a barbecue exists along with the smell of sulfur and a hot breeze on my face. The preserved Word of God paints a more *"vivid"* picture.

KJB – *"Upon the wicked he shall rain snares, fire and brimstone, and an horrible tempest: this shall be the portion of their cup."*

Now I see traps set up by the devil, plenty of fire, a *"horrible"* scorching wind.

Note: The preserved Word of God says that this will be a *"portion"* of their cup. In other words, it is going to get *worse*. Now I am concerned. It is going to be so bad in hell that the Scriptures tell us that people will actually *"pray"* in hell, but not in the NIV. Look up Luke 16:27:

NIV – *"He answered, then I beg you, father, send Lazarus to my father's house."*

KJB – *"Then he said, I pray thee therefore, father, that thou wouldest send him to my father's house."*

Maybe we better get our praying done while we live on the earth because the preserved Word of God in English tells us that we will be *praying* if we go to hell. We tend to pray when our backs are up against the wall don't we? If I were to go to hell, (which thanks to Jesus I am not), I would rather that you not *"pity"* me by saying, *"poor Sal."* I would rather that I can gain *"mercy"* (which of course I would not be able to obtain.) The NIV would rather that you just be *"pitied"* as Luke 16:24 shows us.

NIV – *"So he called to him, Father Abraham, have pity on me and send Lazarus to dip the tip of his finger in water and cool my tongue, because I am in agony in this fire."*

KJB – *"And he cried and said, Father Abraham, have mercy on me, and send Lazarus, that he may dip the tip of his finger in water, and cool my tongue; for I am tormented in the flame."*

I can tolerate being in agony over something for a while. The NIV does not specify if this agony is going to be consistent. But by using the word *"tormented"* the KJB shows that this *torment* is going to *continue*. The words that God chose are always correct. God's choice of words makes sense and is always right the *first time.* Why do these scholars attempt to *correct* God?

Let's see how the choice of words describes the *"severity"* of ones situation. Look up Matt. 13:42:

NIV – *"They will throw them into the fiery furnace, where there will be weeping and gnashing of teeth."*

KJB – *"And shall cast them into a furnace of fire: there shall be wailing and gnashing of teeth."*

The dictionary describes *wailing* as one who makes a long, loud, sad cry, as in grief or pain. I have *wept* in my life for about 3 minutes or less. I have cried many times but not for long periods of time. *"Wailing"* gives me the picture of *"buckets of water."* Wailing is the definition of a real *"cry baby."* Now I can see why the atheists have no fear of hell.

Hell will be a place of *"sorrows."* We have all experienced *sorrow* in our life. We know *heart pain* and how it feels when someone in our family dies. Our heart hurts when we lose a close friend as well. That pain eventually subsides as time passes. We know that in *heaven* there is *no sorrow at all.* Our heart will never experience that hurt again. The NIV doesn't want you to be reminded of that sorrow in hell. Compare the NIV with the Preserved Word of God in Psalm 18:5:

KJB – *"The sorrows of hell compassed me about: the snares of death prevented me."*

NIV – *"The cords of the grave coiled around me; the snares of death confronted me."*

If I am only in a grave, how can anything hurt me? I'm already dead. The word hell indicates that I am alive. Not only that I am alive, but that I am in *sorrow.* If the snares of death are only *"confronting"* me, maybe I can win the confrontation? The preserved Word of God says that it will *"prevent"* me. *I lose.*

In this last example on hell, I want you to specifically notice how preaching on hell is affected when the God correctors change the Bible.

Look up Mark 9:44, 46, and 48.

Three times within 5 consecutive verses of Scripture, God tells us that *"their worm dieth not, and the fire is not quenched."* The NIV only list this verse one time. As a preacher, if I am using the preserved Word of God, I can warn the people that God has repeated this 3 times within 5 verses and that we should surely *pay attention.* If I am preaching from the NIV, I say no such thing.

The Deity of Christ

The doctrine of the *"Deity of Christ"* is very important to the Scriptures because by understanding the *"Deity,"* we can better understand the *"Godhead."* There is only *one God.* This one God manifest Himself in *three* different ways. He manifests Himself as *Father, Son,* and *Holy Spirit.* All three are *one entity.* All three are the same God. Jesus is not a *"created being"* that a certain God, *other than Himself,* created. Jesus is that God who left the throne of heaven to become a man like us, so He could physically die a human death to take our place as a sacrifice for our sins. God was born in human form, unto Mary, by the power of the Holy Spirit, who Himself, is that same God.

The *"Deity"* of Christ explains to us that Jesus was 100% man while at the same time remaining 100% God. Simply put, Jesus is God. John 1:1 helps us to understand the *Deity of Christ.*

"In the beginning was the Word, the Word was with God, and the Word was God."

All reference to the word *"Word,"* is in reference to Jesus. You can substitute Jesus for the word "Word." This verse is found in the Gospel of John 1:1 in the New World Translation, but note how they change God to *"a God."* The New World translation is the Bible of the Jehovah Witnesses. It is a "new world" translation with some *very old heresies.* How ironic that although the NIV gets this right in John 1:1, it mimics the New World Translation of the Jehovah Witnesses by saying *"a Father"* in I Peter 1:17. Look it up! The devil just put this heresy in a different spot when it comes to the NIV and many other modern Bibles.

Many times in Scripture, Jesus will refer to God because He was talking as a man. It seems like Jesus is talking to someone else and not to Himself as God. It seems like a son is talking to his father. "Son of God" is one of His titles. All of that is true, as it pertains to the 100% man that He is. He is actually talking as a *"man"* to *"himself"* as *God.* When this happens in Scripture, the Bible is attesting to the fact that Jesus was 100% man. If Scripture never were to show Jesus as a man, then we all would be saying that He was *never like us.*

On many occasions this same Scripture also depicts Jesus as God. Therefore we can say that in His *"Deity,"* Jesus is also 100% God. We do not need the NIV and the other modern Bible versions to de-emphasize the Scriptures that depict Jesus as God. Neither do we need the NIV to confuse us any further, because as it is, this could already be difficult to understand. But that is exactly what the *counterfeit Bibles* do. They weaken the many verses that show the balance of the *"deity"* when Jesus is to be shown as God.

Let's look at two Scriptures in particular despite the fact that there are more. I Timothy 3:16 is one of these verses.

KJB – *"And without controversy great is the mystery of godliness: God was manifest in the flesh, justified in the Spirit, seen of angels, preached unto the Gentiles, believed on in the world, received up into glory."*

NIV – *"Beyond all question, the mystery of godliness is great: He appeared in a body, was vindicated by the Spirit, was seen by angels, was preached among the nations, was believed on in the world, was taken up in glory."*

The preserved Word of God in this verse is specifically talking about *God* becoming a man. The NIV renders the pronoun *"he"* and makes you wonder to whom the *"he"* in the verse is talking about. By the way, we all appear in a body. But God was manifest in the flesh. Another crucial verse to the *"divine"* side of Jesus is found in Philippians 2:5-6:

KJB – *"Let this mind be in you, which was also in Christ Jesus: Who, being in the form of God, thought it not robbery to be equal with God:"*

NIV – *"Your attitude should be the same as that of Christ Jesus: Who, being in very nature God, did not consider equality with God something to be grasped."*

I can't quite *grasp* what the NIV is trying to say in this verse. Is Jesus just like God in nature only? Or is Jesus actually equal to God because He is God? In the KJB we do not have any need to *grasp* anything. The Word of God is very clear.

Look up Rev. 1:8-13 on your own. These six verses abound with titles and eternal characteristics of Christ and leave no doubt in the reader's mind that Jesus is the "almighty" of verse eight. It reads that way in the KJB but not in the NIV, and not in many of the other modern Bible versions either.

Christ's Return

A faithful servant of Jesus Christ will always look forward to the promised return of his Saviour. What a day of victory that will be, when Jesus returns to the earth for the second time. There will be a final victory in Christ over all evil. Jesus has already won the war against Satan, Satan's angels, and Satan's followers. But it sure would be nice for us to win a few more battles before the Lord comes back. The Bible has several verses of the promised return of Christ. These verses are verses of hope and they help us to be reminded of Christ's final victory, and to be watchful. Those who are soldiers of Christ are on watch duty. Any attack upon these verses in any way should be exposed. There is such an attack made by the NIV and other counterfeit Bibles in Matt. 25:13. Please compare:

NIV – *"Therefore keep watch, because you do not know the day or the hour."*

KJB – *"Watch therefore, for ye know neither the day nor the hour wherein the Son of man cometh."*

Only the spirit of the devil fears the return of Christ. I am glad I am on His side. The most important part of this verse is not so much that I do not know the day or the hour, *but that our saviour Jesus will return.* That's all I need to be reminded. I guess the NIV and the other modern Bible versions forgot.

Preservation

We began chapter five by looking at the doctrine of Salvation, because Salvation is the most important subject in the world. I want to end chapter six by concluding on the doctrine of preservation, because this is the doctrine that is attacked when it comes to the inerrancy of the Scriptures. We addressed this doctrine both in chapters two and three, but lets look at it a little closer.

Let's compare Psalm 12:6-7 and see how the NIV scholars show that they do not regard the doctrine of preservation of the Scriptures with any *"high regard"* at all.

NIV – *"And the words of the Lord are flawless, like silver refined in a furnace of clay, purified seven times. O Lord, you will keep us safe and protect us from such people forever."*

KJB – *"The words of the Lord are pure words: as silver tried in a furnace of earth, purified seven times. Thou shalt keep them, O Lord, Thou shalt preserve them from this generation for ever."*

In the NIV God does not preserve *"His Word,"* He just *"preserves us."* Just to be sure that I had my Hebrew correct, I asked a local Rabbi in my town to tell me what his Old Testament Hebrew said. He said that the word used in Hebrew was the word *"them,"* and that it refers to the preservation of the Words of God. Therefore, the people can *also* be preserved, but only because the Word is preserved.

How *crafty, sly,* and *tricky* the NIV avoided the doctrine of preservation in this mighty preservation verse. Many Christians who have never done a comparative study will never know what God went through on their behalf to preserve His Word. We cannot let our scholars, Bible professors, denominational leaders, and most importantly our pastors, get away with this lie without the flock having a chance to let the Holy Spirit teach us otherwise.

Conclusion to Chapters Five and Six

The modern Bible versions have come a long way from just fixing a few *"thee's"* and *"thou's."* They weren't authorized by God to touch anything, even the Elizabethan dialect. The *"textual critics"* lied to you all the way to the bank. You have bought all kinds of Bibles not saying the same thing. You have bought study guides and commentaries. You have been encouraged to buy the newest and the latest, most improved Bible that man can design. You even have the *Bible of the month.* But what you no longer have are the precious doctrines that your King James Bible taught you when you were young. You no longer have *inspiration, preservation, inerrancy,* and a *confidence* that the Bible you have in your hand is truly authored by God.

The next generation of Christians will be ignorant of vital points of instruction because the *newer,* more *modern,* and *"greatly improved"* versions will have succeeded in slowly stealing everything you have believed about Christianity. The *"problem text"* that is always solved by comparing *"Scripture with Scripture,"* will no longer contain the *"cross references."* If we lose the foundation of our faith, the Word of God, our final authority in all matters of faith and practice, how much longer will it take before all confidence in the Word of God is destroyed?

Textual criticism is an enemy of the Word of God. It seeks to destroy our belief in inspiration and the preservation of God's *holy, perfect, inerrant* and *infallible Word.* Our pastors have led the way. We didn't ask enough questions or demand that our pastor not preach from a counterfeit Bible. Perhaps we all just didn't care? If it was because we just didn't know, then what are we going to do about this, now that this issue is more to the forefront? It is time for action. We are overdue. A focus on this issue must be initiated by the individual. In chapter nine, a full Biblical game plan is given to the individual, so that a defense of the preserved Word of God can be given. But if you need more evidence of corruption in the Word of God, there are some more comparative verses listed in the next chapter.

Chapter Seven

More Evidence of Corruption
(How much do you need?)

There are many books that are available on the subject of the preserved Word of God in English. It is not the intention of this author to repeat or steal any information that has already been written when it comes to comparative Bible verses. The purpose of this chapter is simply to compile a list, so that the investigative Christian and the Bible College student, who might be reading this book, can have a reference made handy for them to find, and then to study these verses for themselves. These same verses can be found elsewhere in the many books that have already been produced. Comments by these writers have already been made. There is a list of such books that have been made available in the recommended reading section of this book. The student can now be led to the books that were of help to this author.

In these books God has provided the student with a wealth of information that explains the significance of the changes made in the Scriptures. This author does not feel that the comments made by other authors can be said any better than they have already said. *This list is not exhaustive.* It is meant to simply get the ball rolling and to show that there are many problems in the modern Bible versions other than *doctrinal.* The doctrinal problems are bad enough.

This book will list the references in order of the books of the Bible for the student's convenience. The verses will be written out of the King James and compared to the NIV. A question will then be asked for the student to search out an answer. Have fun with the *digging for truth.* You can also use these verses to defend your position as you stand for the preserved Word of God in English, against the textual critics who do not believe in the inerrancy of the Scriptures, and against the pastors who follow them. Let's hope they do not choose to remain blind as you witness to them.

II Samuel 21:19

NIV – *"In another battle with the Philistines at Gob, Elhanan son of Jaare-Oregim the Bethlehemite killed Goliath the Gittite, who had a spear with a shaft like a weaver's rod."*

KJB – *"And there was again a battle in Gob with the Philistines, where Elhanan the son of Jaare-Oregim, a Bethlehemite, slew the brother of Goliath the Gittite, the staff of whose spear was like a weaver's beam."*

Who killed Goliath? (The answer is found in I Samuel 17:45-49.)

Matthew 27:24B

NIV - *"I am innocent of this man's blood, he said. It is your responsibility."*

KJB – *"I am innocent of the blood of this just person: See ye to it."*

Did Pilate think more highly of Jesus than the NIV scholars?

Mark 10:24

NIV – *"The disciples were amazed at his words. But Jesus said again, Children, how hard it is to enter the kingdom of God!"*

KJB – *"And the disciples were astonished at his words. But Jesus answereth again, and saith unto them, Children, how hard is it for them that trust in riches to enter into the kingdom of God!"*

For whom is it hard to enter into the Kingdom of God?

Mark 13:33

NIV – *"Be on guard! Be on alert! You do not know when that time will come."*

KJB – *"Take ye heed, watch and pray: For ye know not when the time is."*
When we are on watch, should we pray?

Luke 2:14
NIV – *"Glory to God in the highest, and on earth, peace to men on whom his favor rests."*
KJB – *"Glory to God in the highest, and on earth "peace, good will toward men."*
Do these two Bibles bear the same witness?

Luke 4:4
NIV – *"Jesus answered, it is written: Man does not live on bread alone."*
KJB – *"And Jesus answered him, saying, It is written, That man shall not live by bread alone, but by every word of God."*
If man cannot live on bread alone, what else does he need?

Luke 4:18
NIV – *"The Spirit of the Lord is on me, because he has anointed me to preach good news to the poor. He has sent me to proclaim freedom for the prisoners and recovery of sight for the blind, to release the oppressed."*
KJB – *"The Spirit of the Lord is upon me, because he hath anointed me to preach the gospel to the poor; he hath sent me to heal the broken hearted, to preach deliverance to the captives, and recovering of sight to the blind, to set at liberty them that are bruised."*
Does Jesus have anything in His ministry for the broken hearted?

Luke 8:48
NIV – *"Then he said to her, Daughter, your faith has healed you. Go in peace."*
KJB – *"And he said unto her, Daughter, be of good comfort: Thy faith hath made thee whole; go in peace."*
Does Jesus wish to comfort us?

Luke 9:55
NIV – *"But Jesus turned and rebuked them."*
KJB – *"But he turned, and rebuked them, and said, Ye know not what manner of spirit ye are of."*
What spirit do you think the modern day Bible scholars are of?

Luke 22:64

NIV – *"They blindfolded him and demanded, "Prophesy! Who hit you?""*

KJB – *"And when they had blindfolded him, they struck him on the face, and asked him, saying, Prophesy who is it that smote thee?"*

Where did they hit Jesus?

Luke 23:42

NIV – *"Then he said, Jesus, remember me when you come into your kingdom."*

KJB – *"And he said unto Jesus, Lord, remember me when thou comest into thy kingdom."*

Did the "Divine Christ" abandon the "man" Jesus when he was hanging on the cross?"

John 1:18

NIV – *"No one has ever seen God, but God the One and Only, who came from the Father, full of grace and truth."*

KJB – *"No man hath seen God at any time, the only begotten Son, which is in the bosom of the Father, he hath declared him."*

How many Gods are there?

John 3:16

NIV – *"For God so loved the world that he gave his one and only Son, that whoever believes in him shall not perish but have eternal life."*

KJB – *"For God so loved the world that he gave his only begotten Son, that whosoever believeth in him should not perish, but have everlasting life."*

Are those of us who are saved, also considered Sons of God? (The answer is found in John 1:12 and in other verses.)

John 6:47

NIV – *"I tell you the truth, he who believes has everlasting life."*

KJB – *"Verily, verily, I say unto you, He that believeth on me hath everlasting life."*

If you believe in anything that you want, is it good enough to save you? (The answer is found in James 2:19.)

John 6:69

NIV – *"We believe and know that you are the Holy One of God."*

KJB – *"And we believe and are sure that thou art that Christ, the Son of the living God."*

Is God living today?

Acts 7:37

NIV – *"This is that Moses who told the Israelites, God will send you a prophet like me from your own people."*

KJB – *"This is that Moses, which said unto the children of Israel, A prophet shall the Lord your God raise up unto you of your brethren, like unto me; him shall ye hear."*

Do the NIV scholars want to hear anything about the controversy concerning the Scriptures?

Romans 11:6

NIV – *"And if by grace, then it is no longer by works; if it were, grace would no longer be grace."*

KJB – *"And if by grace, then is it no more of works: otherwise grace is no more grace. But if it be of works, then is it no more grace: otherwise work is no more work."*

Does the second part of this verse address works when it comes to Salvation?

I Corinthians 5:7B

NIV – *"Christ, our Passover lamb, has been sacrificed."*

KJB – *"For even Christ our Passover is sacrificed for us."*

Christ was sacrificed for whom?

II Corinthians 2:17

NIV – *"Unlike so many, we do not peddle the word of God for profit. On the contrary, in Christ we speak before God with sincerity, like men sent from God."*

KJB – *"For we are not as many, which corrupt the word of God: but as of sincerity, but as of God, in the sight of God speak we in Christ."*

Do you think the modern Bible scholar actually peddles, and corrupts, the Word of God for profit at the same time?

Gal. 3:1

NIV – *"You foolish Galatians! Who has bewitched you? Before your eyes Jesus Christ was clearly portrayed as crucified."*

KJB – *"O foolish Galatians, who hath bewitched you, that ye should not obey the truth, before whose eyes Jesus Christ hath been evidently set forth, crucified among you."*

What has the devil bewitched us into *not* obeying?

Philippians 3:16

NIV – *"Only let us live up to what we have already attained."*

KJB – *"Nevertheless, whereto we have already attained, let us walk by the same rule, let us mind the same thing."*

Is minding over 200 different Bible versions in English walking by the same rule and minding the same thing?

I Timothy 6:5

NIV – *"And constant friction between men of corrupt minds, who have been robbed of the truth and who think that godliness is a means to financial gain."*

KJB – *"Perverse disputings of men of corrupt minds, and destitute of the truth, supposing that gain is godliness: from such withdraw thyself."*

Should we hang around any college, denomination or pastor who preaches from an untruthful counterfeit Bible?

I John 4:3A

NIV – *"But every spirit that does not acknowledge Jesus is not from God."*

KJB – *"And every spirit that confesseth not that Jesus Christ is come in the flesh is not of God."*

Did God manifest Himself in the flesh in the person of Jesus?

Rev. 14:5

NIV – *"No lie was found in their mouths; they are blameless."*

KJB – *"And in their mouth was found no guile: for they are without fault before the throne of God."*

They are without fault before what?

Rev. 22:14

NIV – *"Blessed are those who wash their robes, that they may have the right to the tree of life and may go through the gates into the city."*

KJB – *"Blessed are they that do His commandments, that they may have right to the tree of life, and may enter in through the gates into the city."*

Are you blessed when you wash your robe?

Hard Words versus Easy Words
(Are the modern versions easier to read?)

One of the strongest arguments that the modern Bible scholar uses to justify their destruction of the Bible is that their versions are easier to *read* and easier to *understand*. The facts prove that this excuse, to make money on their invention, is not true. The King James Bible is a 5th grade reading level, and the NIV is an 8th grade reading level. Science refutes that claim in the other versions as well. The NASB is a 6th grade reading level and the NKJV is a 7th grade reading level. If the Bible was easier to read and easier to understand since 1881, shouldn't Christianity be doing better? In America, have we gotten better in our morality or worse since 1881? We have gone downhill since 1881.

Surely the age of Laodicea has been ushered in sometime after 1881. This is the year when Westcott and Hort wrote the Greek Text that underlies the modern Bible versions. Unlike the age of Philadelphia, we abandoned the preserved Word of God. There will not be a blessing for our disobedience. Forget about a revival or be willing to change back to God's Word. Don't hold your breath that your pastor will lead the way. You do it!

Another argument of the modern Bible scholar is that it was necessary to upgrade the King James Bible because the King James Bible had too many *"archaic words."* There are archaic words in the King James Bible. This is true, but so what? Who put these archaic words in the Bible, and who instructs us to leave them right where He put them? God instructs us, in His Word, how to deal with archaic words. Dr. Sam Gipp addresses archaic words in the Bible in his book, *Gipp's Understandable History of the Bible.*

Found on pages 64-66 of this book is a great rundown of I Samuel chapter 9 where God shows an archaic word *"seer"* that was updated to *"prophet"* right in the text. Later on in the passage, God leaves the word that He chose *"seer,"* right in the *same text.* This is what He shows us to do as well. Did he give us another game plan after 1881?

Leave God's choice of words alone. We have not been authorized by God to change a single thing in His Word. There have been no improvements in our modern choice of words. Most of these new choices of words have more syllables than the King James Word. When you do not understand an archaic word, use a dictionary and increase your vocabulary.

Here are three examples of what we would call an archaic word in the KJB.

Shambles… This word means "market place."

Peradventure… This word means "by chance."

Furlong… This word means "mile."

All these words and other words are Modern English Words. They do have an older dialect, but these words are in our Modern English Dictionary. God says to leave them alone.

The facts show that there are more HARD words in the NIV than EASY words in the King James Bible. Archaic words are not limited to the King James Bible. Not only do the modern Bible versions often retain the supposedly archaic word in the King James Bible, but many times a more formidable word is used to correct a perfectly understandable word or phrase in the King James Bible.

The following list of harder words in the NIV is taken from the 560 page, intensive and detailed work entitled *Archaic Words and the Authorized Version,* by Dr. Lawrence M. Vance. With permission, I have reproduced a very small portion of this work to show that the NIV is not easier to read and to understand. Compare these HARD WORDS in the NIV, to the EASY WORD chosen by God in the King James Bible.

Here is a list of some of the more interesting comparisons:

NIV	BIBLE VERSE	KJB
Acclimation	II Chron. 15:14	Voice
Alcove	Ezek. 40:13	Little Chamber
Annotations	II Chron. 13:22	Story
Blustering	Job 8:2	Strong
Fomenting	Isaiah 59:13	Speaking
Brood	Isaiah 57:4	Children
Cooing	Song 2:12	Voice
Curds	Gen 18:8	Butter
Detachment	John 18:3	Band
Dissipation	I Pet. 4:4	Riot
Goiim	Gen. 14:1	Nations
Impaled	Ezra 6:11	Hanged
Infamy	Isaiah 44:11	Ashamed
Mina	Luke 19:16	Pound
Misdemeanor	Acts 18:14	Wrong
Negev	Gen. 12:9	South
Nephilim	Gen. 6:4	Giants
Oblivion	Psalm 88:12	Forgetfulness
Porphyry	Ester 1:6	Red
Portent	Isaiah 20:3	Wonder
Portico	I Kings 6:3	Porch
Sachet	Song 1:13	Bundle
Torrent	Rev. 12:15	Flood
Verdant	Song 1:16	Green
Wadi	Numbers 34:5	River[19]

Dr. Vance has over 250 of these comparisons. The claim that the modern Bible versions are easier to read and to understand is a great selling tactic that you bought with your hard earned money. The scholars, the publishing companies, and the so-called Christian bookstores are laughing all the way to the bank. They have your money in their hand. Your pastor has put these versions in the church pew and he reads them from the pulpit. We, the people, let him get away with it. Once again it is time for a Bible "tea party."

---

19. Vance, Lawrence. *Archaic Words and the Authorized Version.* (Vance Publications: Pensacola, FL, 2011)

We Talk Like a King James Bible

The modern day scholar says that the King James Bible has too many *"archaic words."* It is written in an *"old and archaic language"* that we cannot understand. This was the reason, and the excuse, that was rendered by these scholars, so that they could make money on the new Bibles that they produced. They disobeyed the Lord's last command. They claimed that they were only going to update these "archaic words." Even if updating these archaic words was all that they did, they would still be in disobedience, because God told us to leave the so called "outdated words" alone. (Read first Samuel chapter 9.) We must *not* fix the "thee's and thou's." This is disobedience against God.

They used this excuse to change the many doctrines that we hold dear. *However, there are many modern day sayings that come directly from the King James Bible.* Hundreds can be presented, but we will limit ourselves to just twenty. We will take 10 from the Old Testament and 10 from the New Testament. The King James Bible is written in *modern* English, which is dated around 1400 A.D. to the present day. It is accused of being "old English." The dates of "old English" are about 400 A.D. – 1050 A.D. "mid English" is about 1050 A.D. to 1400 A.D.

The following is only part of a list found on the website www.av1611.org. This shows many modern day sayings which come from the KJB. Even though they are not "word for word" our sayings' roots come from the KJB.

Old Testament

1. Genesis 4:2-5 "can't get blood from a turnip."
2. Exodus 19:16-18 "holy smoke."
3. Exodus 32:8 "holy cow."
4. Deuteronomy 2:14 "wasted him."
5. Deuteronomy 32:10 "apple of his eye."
6. Judges 5:20 "star wars."
7. I Samuel 14:12 "I'll show you a thing or two."
8. I Kings 3:7 "don't know if he is coming or going."
9. II Chronicles 9:6 "you haven't heard half of it."
10. Proverbs 18:6 "he is asking for it."

1.   Matthew 25:1-10 "burning the midnight oil."
2.   Matthew 25:33 "right or left side of an issue."
3.   Matthew 27:46 "for crying out loud."
4.   Mark 5:13 "hog wild."
5.   Luke 11:46 "won't lift a finger to help."
6.   Luke 15:17 "he came to himself."
7.   Romans 2:23 "breaking the law."
8.   Philippians 3:2 "beware of dog."
9.   Colossians 2:14 "they nailed him"
10.   Matthew 2:1 "what a wise guy."[20]

Comments on Chapter 7

There are many more verses that could have been written down in this chapter. Over 64,000 words have been changed or omitted in the counterfeit Bibles. This has affected over 5,778 verses in the Bible. The church no longer believes in the inerrancy of Scripture. No one has the right to meddle with the Word of God. Our security and faith in God's ability to preserve the Scriptures is threatened. This apostasy from within is causing God to ignore our cries for revival. He cannot visit us, and bring power back to the church, as long as we *disobey* Him.

We let our leaders do that to us, because we are blind and indifferent towards the truth. This generation is full of opinions. The truth of this generation is subjective. God's truth is no longer absolute. Let it be impressed upon our conscience that we will always be dependent upon the Scriptures in all matters of faith and practice. No revival can survive and make an indelible mark upon history without the perfectly, preserved, Word of God.

The church has no business disobeying the last command of Jesus. The cries for revival should cease if there continues to be a disregard for the changing of God's Word. The church no longer clings to the flawless instruction of the Bible. Yet it deceives the flock into thinking that it does. If the church does not admit to its sins in this matter, then the future for revival is bleak. We deserve the severest chastisement of our Lord. Be assured that God will have the last say

---

20. Fighting Back! A Handy Reference for King James Bible Believers: *Seventy-Five Common Sayings.* <http://www.av1611.org/jmelton/fight. html#fight4/> (Accessed 08/05/11)

in this matter at the judgment. Although Jesus has won the war, it sure would be nice to take back some battles on our watch.

The alternative is to sit by and *say nothing,* and to sit by and *do nothing.* That would really please the devil, the Roman Catholic Church, and anyone who is making money on your indifference. Each of us should drill a hole into the middle of our modern Bible and mail it back to the publishing companies, with a note attached to it, explaining the reason you no longer want their product. Your pastor should be the first person to do this. This should be an issue for the Board of Directors of the church. You take the lead. No one else will.

Chapter Eight

Let's Talk About Revival

Try asking any Christian that you know this question. Do you want to see a revival in the church today? Every single one of them would say "yes." *Everybody* is talking about the need for revival. *Everybody* wants *somebody* to do something about revival, but *nobody* is doing *anything*, that is making a *difference in history*. There are a few Bible believing Christians who are out there defending the Preserved Word of God, and who have solid Bible doctrine. They preach against sin and preach Salvation by Grace through Faith, but, by and large, *it is not getting done*.

How Do We Know That We Need a Repentance/Revival?

The *presence* of the "Holy Spirit" seems to have gone.
The number of *"decisions for Christ"* is down.
Churches have become more *"social"* than *"evangelistic."*
Most churches are no longer functioning as an *"organism."*
They are functioning as an *"organization"* instead.

Most *"bus ministries"* that used to reach out to the inner city, no longer operate.

Many churches are *stuck* in their ways, unable to be used of God.

The music sounds more and more like *"rock and roll."*

Church attendance is down in most every denomination.

Damnable *heresies* and *false doctrines* have found their way into the church.

Most of these churches are using a *"COUNTERFEIT BIBLE."*

The Persecution of Our Own Brothers and Sisters

The faithful Christians who stand for the preserved Word of God are under great persecution by their own brothers and sisters in Christ, who are doing everything that they can to divide us in our Bible, and who support the evil spirit of modern Bible scholarship. These Christians, who persecute, are the biggest *hindrance* to a *repentance* that would allow God to move in history, and to send a revival to His church in the 21st Century. Only a handful of faithful warriors are left, and there are only a few troops in the ranks. They need you! Where do you stand? Can you face this Goliath with a few stones in your hand? What is your game plan?

The Cost of a Repentance/Revival

We have no idea what a revival is going to cost us. I am not confident that we know what it will take for a true revival to be a *reality*. We should be more honest with ourselves and stop talking about revival all together, unless we are serious about *paying* the price for this revival. I do not believe that we want a revival. Do you think the majority of Christians are really serious about a revival? The evidence of any desire for a revival is obviously not there. If we really wanted a revival, we would be paying more attention to the controversy concerning our Bible. If we wanted a revival, we would call the use of counterfeit Bibles exactly what it is, and that is *sin*.

In order for a repentance/revival to break out, *at the least,* these following three things must happen. Then, maybe God will lead us to some other problems that also need to be changed.

1. **Leadership must be willing to allow God to correct and change, the way it has become.** Christian *scholars* and *professors* in our *colleges*, along with *denominational leaders* and *pastors*, must repent for promoting the preaching of false doctrines, and for their support of COUNTERFEIT BIBLES in our churches. Some have *purposefully* misled the people. These are the men we have followed. They are the ones who are leading the church. *Leadership* is accountable to God and *responsible* for the people.

2. **False teaching must be exposed both in/out of the church.** Inwardly we must get back to *Biblical* doctrine which has been made out to be *nonessential* and *unnecessary*. Unity has become a higher value than *truth*. We rather compromise then cause any division. The Bible says otherwise.

We must teach our people how to deal with the false teaching of *Roman Catholicism, Mormonism, The Jehovah Witnesses, Islam,* and other *false Religions* like *Freemasonry*. *Marxism* is very influential within our *educational system* and it must be exposed. *Marxism* has infiltrated our *political system* as well. We are losing the battle to many of these groups, because Christians do not choose to defend their beliefs. Many Christians do not know *how* to defend their beliefs. As a result, the Freemasons are influencing the *New World Order* which will bring about a "**A one world church along with a one world government.**" (II Thessalonians 2:3-4.)

The *Freemasons* operate within the *Democratic Party,* as well as the *Republican Party*. True Christians are no longer represented by either party. A little evil is just as bad as a lot of evil. Our churches have allowed the Freemasons to *infiltrate* the church from *within*. Many of our pastors hold the 33rd degree and many *Freemasons* are allowed to sit on the *Board of Directors* of their church. The masons know who we are *but we do not know who they are*. What's the secret?

3. **Most importantly, and as top priority, there must be a massive return to the preserved word of God in English, which is the King James Bible.** This must be done in *obedience to God*. Many Christians are using a counterfeit Bible unaware. The *truth* must be told to the average person who does not realize that *leadership* has lied, *"perhaps unintentionally,"* and that many *leaders* who profess to be Christians, (but have become apostate) are holding hands with THE ROMAN CATHOLIC CHURCH. They stay silent when it comes to talking about how the preserved Word of God in English has been changed.

They keep the people uninformed. As far as revival is concerned, the *most important issue* facing the church is *"its own Bible."*

How the church will deal with the cancer of *"counterfeit Bibles,"* within its own house, may determine whether a spark of *"revival"* can come back to the church, so that the true church, which is made up of people who are saved, is able to bring our country back to the *"ways of God."* It will take the church and not the Republican party to accomplish this goal.

If we really wanted a revival, we would stand against the false spirit of modern Bible scholarship, and the spirit of error in our lives. There is no effective strategy for a return to the preserved Word of God. We should be more concerned about the errors in our doctrines, and be more studious as to what we believe. We sit and say nothing when it comes to the truth concerning this issue. Except for the few brave troops that are left, no one is saying anything about the spirit of modern Bible scholarship. The devil runs rampant. Our pastors are getting away with preaching from these counterfeit Bibles, and we are not challenging them to change. If using counterfeit Bibles is *not a sin,* then neither is *disobedience a sin.*

Revival must be granted to us by God. It is not our right to have revival, just drop into our lap. It is a privilege to have the blessing of God in the age that we live. The Holy Spirit brings revival when each one of us personally repents. Great change must occur. *The norm must be strongly interrupted.* A forgiven dependence upon God must be desired. This must be happening in many individuals simultaneously. The prophet Habakkuk prayed this beautiful prayer in Habakkuk 3:2:

"O' Lord, I have heard thy speech, and was afraid: O Lord, revive thy work in the midst of the years, in the midst of the years make known; in wrath remember mercy."

Habakkuk heard God's speech. The word of God was active and alive in his heart. The word of God affected him, and he was afraid. He knew the Lord was not pleased. He knew, first of all, that *he must change.* He also knew that there must be a change in others around him. *Habakkuk was aware and alerted to sin.* No one ever calls it a sin for a preacher to preach from a counterfeit Bible. It is not condemned. Yet, this is an *abomination* before God. God is woefully displeased. But since we are not seeking His blessing, and we do not really desire a revival, we cannot see this displeasure in God. We are blind Laodiceans. We are naked, because of our blindness. There is no change in sight. Rev. 4:11 says this…

"Thou art worthy, O Lord, to receive glory and honour and power: for thou hast created all things, and for thy pleasure they are and were created."

God is the creator of His Word. Remember, God magnifies His Word even above all His Name. (Psalm 138:2.) *We sin* when we *disobey* His last command to leave His Word alone. We were not to change a single word when the Bible was finally purified in English for the seventh time. We allowed the Roman Catholic Jesuits to infiltrate our Bible. It is the Final Authority of the Bible, that exposes the false doctrines of the Roman Catholic Church, even to this day. So if you do not want to do battle with the Roman Catholic Jesuits, then be honest and admit that you are not praying for any revival to happen. If you do want to see a revival happen in the age that you live, then be willing to pay the cost of returning to the preserved Word of God, and prepare for a great *spiritual war.*

If the people are not reached with the *truth,* we will continue to move away from God. We will forfeit God's Blessing, there will not be a repentance/revival in our time. What do you, *a member of the flock,* want to do about this? How should you respond to a *pastor* who is not *listening,* and who is not *teaching* and *preaching* from the Bible that came from God?

Hopefully, this book will be a starting point in showing the average Christian that most *pastors* are preaching from a Bible that comes from so called *"scholars,"* who have changed God's preserved Word for *"money and political correctness."* Some of these pastors could be in fear of losing their jobs. Nonetheless, our scholars and pastors allow *education* to promote *"textual criticism."* They have become *"correctors of God."* They choose to worship *"education."* Their own education has become an idol to them.

God delights in the Word that He gave to us. He has perfectly preserved His Word and it is available to us in English to this day. We are not revived because we have not repented for using something other than His preserved Word. There has not been a true revival in the church any time after Westcott and Hort changed the preserved Greek text in 1881. We ourselves prevent God from extending the privilege to visit us in the age of Laodicea. We prevent Him from sending us a revival. Be honest, how much are you praying for a real awakening to happen? Are you willing to pay the price that it will cost?

False Revival in 21st Century America

Some people are claiming that a revival is already happening. *The so called revival that we see today is not of God.* It has made no indelibly mark upon history, and it has not changed the culture of our sinful society. There is a lot of emotion shown in some church services where people are jumping and hollering all over the place. Quite frankly, it is bizarre in its behavior. There is also a lot of *unbiblical* preaching concerning money. Rich radio and T.V. evangelists are lining their pockets with fund raisers. They have become professional *money makers.* They preach a false *"prosperity gospel."* Some are simply, *"feel good preachers."*

They are not changing anything in the big scheme of things. The bars are not closing like they did in the days of Spurgeon, and others, like Jonathan Edwards. The casinos are not being voted "against" when we vote on whether or not to have a casino in our communities. The prostitute houses are a lucrative business that thrives. Some of these pastors have made a visit or two to these houses themselves.

Abortion continues to kill over a million babies a year in the United States. The Republican Party knows how to make a lot of money on this issue. We need to lose that money and *win the issue.* Do you think the church will be powerful enough to overturn Roe vs. Wade? Today's truth is subjective, and our opinions take the place of God's absolute truth. The confusion in the Christian Bible will have no power to change this behavior. Have you ever been to a Bible study where different Bible versions are used? Were you able to follow without doing a double take?

The so-called *"salt of the earth"* does its own thing within the walls of a church, and does not even know or care about the spiritual condition of their next door neighbor. *"Come to the church,"* and we will feed you *our way.* There is nothing wrong with going to church, but there is something wrong with the way we are being fed.

There are not many visitation teams going out to the lost. There are rare visits to the neighborhood by the church, where an invitation to the people is extended for them to attend. You may say nobody answers their door anymore, but they will know the *genuine Christians* by their love. (John 13:35.) If we show that love in their neighborhood, they will be much more inclined to listen. God will be with those who stand on His preserved Word, as they share the truth in love. God's Word will never return void. (Isaiah 55:11) To be obedient, it has to be God's Word, *not* a counterfeit, then His Word can work as promised. As it stands now, if new people come to your church, you have to wonder if the truth of Salvation is going to be preached, along with sound biblical doctrine from God's preserved Bible.

There are plenty of ministers with no real ministry. It is all about the *"money,"* instead of the *"gospel."* They usually wait for you to show up. It is more about you *outreaching* for a ministry instead of a ministry that extends an *outreach to you.* You have to become a member before you are shown any real attention. Pay your tithes and do not ask any tough, honest questions. If you discern the wrong spirit, do not cause division by your questioning of that spirit. Do not question the Bible that your pastor is using. Make no waves and stay ignorant. Just become a team player and be a follower of all that your church believes. What happened to the gift of discernment?

Beware of the pastor who condescends down to you and makes you feel intimidated. His education and his study on "textual criticism" have made him a corrector of God. He might even have an air of arrogance about him. No pastor should have a mind control over you. Preaching the Word of God to you does not render to the pastor the right to have power and control over your right to discern the truth of God. The Holy Spirit lives in you and He will guide you into all truth. Follow your pastor only if he is following God.

Beware of *false doctrines* in the church of the unchangeable pastor. If he has a counterfeit Bible, he is probably preaching some wrong doctrine that lines up with that counterfeit. You get wrong teaching and a false sense of personal holiness. All of a sudden you believe certain things like this:

You cannot possibly be saved unless you speak in tongues.

You cannot take medicine and be a person of faith.

You must be spiritual if you are materially blessed.

It is your lack of faith if you are not physically healed.

If you do not speak in tongues, then you have no evidence of the Holy Spirit living in your life.

The truth of God is constantly evolving.

Handle a snake, then you are a man of faith.

The Holy Spirit will zap you into submission.

You can confess your sins to a priest.

Mary, the mother of Jesus, was sinless.

Pay a priest for a mass to get your dead relative out of Purgatory.

If you are wearing a scapular when you die, you will be saved.

Jesus is literally present in a wafer.

Christians in heaven can make intercession for you.

Water Baptism is essential for you to be saved.

Giving money to God will pay you back in monetary dividends.

There are many more false doctrines that can be listed. False teaching in the name of Christianity is present everywhere. People are told that they can lose their Salvation and that Salvation can be attained by "Good Works," and that Salvation can be maintained by *"holy living."* Holy Living is certainly a big part of the Christian experience, but the Holiest person alive still has a sinful nature and can never live a perfect life on earth. Most of the holiness denominations are using a counterfeit Bible. Isn't that unholy?

Isaiah 64:6 says:

"But we are all as an unclean thing, and all our righteousnesses are as filthy rags; and we all do fade as a leaf; and our iniquities, like the wind, have taken us away."

Should We Give Up?

Is it too late? After all, the majority of Christians do not use God's preserved Word in English, but they have made the switch to a COUNTERFEIT Bible, because they have followed their pastor. Should we just give up, or should we "fight on?" Is it possible that most pastors, and most of the people, did not know about this? Are people telling you that this subject doesn't matter? Or could it be that the *blindness* of the Laodician church has it so firmly in its grip, that our pastors and the people themselves, will do nothing about this situation?

Can one individual really make a difference? The author of this book believes that the answer to these questions is YES! We should *"fight on."* And YES! One individual can make a difference. *Gideon* was one man who was mighty in valor. *Elijah*, who prayed that it would *not rain*, and who *defeated* the prophets of *Baal*, was another. Many other Bible heroes showed what one individual can achieve. Like *Esther*, we are here for such a time as this. These biblical examples were so timely uttered by one of my ministries board members, attorney Doug Fowler.

Even though most people do not know what has been done to the Bible, it is not too late to do something about this situation. It not only *matters* it is *imperative* that we do something about this situation. Think about what *"we the people"* can do. Nowhere in the book of Revelation do we read that a repentance/revival cannot break out in the age of Laodicea. But in order to get God's attention we must get back to the *"WORD OF THE COVENANT."*

The average Christian must be equipped with enough basic information so that he/she will be able to have an intelligent discussion with his/her pastor on the issue of *Counterfeit Bibles in English,* and what it is going to take for a *repentance/revival to break out among Christians.* If the *people* help their pastor to *change,* we can *get God's attention* because *"we the people"* will once again be following God in this *vital area.* Most people have never done a *"comparative"* Bible study on their own. Most people do not *know* or *understand* the cost of a *repentance/revival.* We Laodicians defend: The devil, our errant pastors, and our pastors "alma mater," without investigating this issue with an open mind toward what is *true.*

The church is in desperate need of a *"Bible tea party,"* which must be led by the individual. Leadership will either have to *change* or be *replaced.* The *flock* must hold leadership *accountable* for not making the necessary changes that will spark a much needed renewal within the church. Failure to do so will cause the church to continue to move in a direction that is moving *away from God* and closer to the *Antichrist.* The line has been drawn in the sand. We have no choice but to go one way or the other. Which way are you heading?

The Greatest Hindrance to a Repentance/Revival

If you were to ask your pastor what the greatest hindrance to revival is in this day we live, he would probably say *"unbelief."* I believe that this is true. Not believing God at His Word leads to all kinds of disobedience. But one of the most serious problems is right *under our nose.* The problem in our own Bible, and the *confusion* that the enemy has ushered in, with our permission, is the *number one reason we do not have a revival in our time.* Did we not believe God when he said he would preserve His Word for us? Why the questioning concerning the completed Bible in English? God used the purest dialect in

English, at His ordained time, and brought us a Bible that *rhymes, sings,* is *poetic* and has *alliteration* in it. We didn't change Shakespeare did we? Can you imagine Shakespeare being changed into our modern dialect? If we changed Shakespeare, it would no longer be a classic.

Has God foreordained us to be locked into the predicament that we find ourselves in the age of Laodicea? Absolutely not!

Many people believe, that because the ship is sinking, and that certain things are inevitable in Bible prophecy, that we are to sit back and do nothing. The very opposite of this belief is what we should be doing.

We should not allow the inevitable *to happen on our watch.* Instead of sitting back and anticipating more apostasy, we should let a personal revival *happen inside of us.* We should refuse to let the devil win this battle. If enough individuals start praying for the same thing, and put some feet to their prayers, the number game will start to change, and the power of many people who think alike, and who have the truth inside of them, will once again make a difference in how we act out our beliefs. Change will come and it will force the devil to go to another game plan. Think about how many people could get saved in the meantime?

If Bible prophecy is being fulfilled under your watch and my watch, (and it is) *then we are the problem.* Look at what it says in Luke 18:8.

"I tell you that he will avenge them speedily. Nevertheless when the Son of man cometh, shall he find faith on the earth?"

Because of the sinfulness of the times, there is a tendency toward "unbelief." We must believe that God will raise the standard. We must ask ourselves if we will be part of that standard or if we will be a hindrance to that standard because of the inevitable? We must preach the truth of His Word because in modern times we have replaced His Word with a *Crossless Christ, with no blood in redemption,* and plenty of *feel good religion.* We are not seeing strong Christians with plenty of faith in God. Yet in John 8:30-32 it says:

"As he spake these words, many believed on him." Then said Jesus to those Jews which believed on him, If ye continue in my word, then are ye my disciples indeed; And ye shall know the truth, and the truth shall set you free."

The truth is what will set us free. But we must want to continue in God's preserved Word in English, the King James Bible. Modern Bible scholarship has lied to us and it has taken our money. It has exchanged the truth of God for a lie. It sold us the *best, new improved,* more *modern* and the easier to *read and to understand* line. We took it hook, line, and sinker. Madison Avenue has our money and we will still be looking for the next *"Bible of the month."*

The answer to our own question of revival is right under our nose. It is a return to the preserved word of God in English, the King James Bible. When and if we do this, we will put God back into the position of being able to bless us. This will only happen if a revival burns inside of *"we the people."* Our leadership is not going in that direction. You have to be strong enough spiritually in this disturbing issue to change your leadership.

Any believer who has grown cold will need to honestly go before God and repent. We need to return to our first love as the Bible instructs us to do in Revelation 2:1-7. If we ask God to point out where the starting point of repentance should be, He will point us to His Word. Don't study the version of that Word, which has been butchered by the scholars and the pastors that they taught, or you will never get back to the starting point that is right under your nose.

The preserved Word of God is available to us by the promise of God and we are not using it. We must change what has been going on for the last 130 years. We must change this disobedience and admit to ourselves that this is sin. If we see this as sin, and if we repent, we will give God the chance to visit us afresh. A powerful church, united on one Bible, can bring this country back to the basic Bible beliefs that made us great. I will close this chapter with this very well *quoted,* but not often *obeyed* verse in II Chronicles 7:14.

"If my people, which are called by my name, shall humble themselves, and pray, and seek my face, and turn from their wicked ways; then will I hear from heaven, and will forgive their sin, and will heal their land."

If my people... Those who are saved.

Which are called by my name... Christians.

Shall humble themselves... Admit that there is a problem.

And pray... Bring God back into the picture.

And seek my face... Get God's viewpoint and help.

And turn from their wicked ways... Repent for disobeying God's commandments.

Then I will hear from heaven... We will get God's attention.

And will forgive their sin... Give us a new start.

And will heal their land… Send a revival to the church.

If we refuse to turn from our wicked ways, God cannot forgive our sin. And our land will not be healed. How much do we want to see a true revival in our lifetime, that will make an indelible mark on history?

Chapter Nine

So What Should We Do?

Now that you have looked into this issue, what should you do? You certainly do not want to be the cause of any problem. You do not want to cause division in your church. Christians do not like conflict. Unfortunately, the problem is already here and it is 130 years old. Is there a solution? Can we really be a part of a great repentance/revival and move God to visit us? Does anyone have a game plan? What steps can we take to unify the body of Christ on the final authority of God's Word? You certainly do not want to stand there and do nothing. So what can you do? What should you do?

I want to make several suggestions as to what you can and should do. One thing is for certain. Do not stand by and do nothing. The battle is yours and your neighbor's. Counterfeit Bibles affect us all. One way or another, you will be a weaker Christian for having said *"nothing."* Here are some suggestions as you journey to defend the preserved Word of God:

Pray For The Truth To Be Revealed To You
If you were to follow my experience in this issue, you

were not aware of what had happened and how your Bible was changed. I got alone with God, and with a desire to know the truth, I began to *pray* that God would reveal His truth to me, because I was hearing too much information that was not making any sense. After studying the view point of the preserved Word, I realized that another view point was saying that God never preserved His Word and none of us are able to find it. We either had the preserved Word of God available to us or we just had a bunch of Bibles that were a scattered collection of the truth.

The wrong view said the Bible was not in one place to be found, but scattered everywhere in a conglomeration of different Bibles not saying the same thing. Mind you, the Bible had delivered me from the indoctrination of Roman Catholicism for the first 19 years of my life. I never even knew where the books of the Bible were, until I got saved and began to read it. The final authority, of the Bible, is all that I had that gave me confidence to know the truth of God, in all matters of faith and practice.

If the Bible wasn't real, then perhaps my conversion was not real either, and perhaps my upbringing was right after all? Without the truth of the Bible, I would have remained a Roman Catholic.

The latter reasoning did not sound like God to me. For me to go back to Catholicism was out of the question. I wanted to know, *from a spiritual point of view,* what was the correct answer. I wanted to know the truth concerning this issue. I had built a 16-team NIV Bible quiz league. I felt a great responsibility to *do the right thing* in the eyes of God. In my prayers I told God that I would surely take the responsibility of being wrong if I could only have the *truth.* I was willing to make the truth hurt.

That 16 team Bible quiz league was *my little baby.* It took years of hard work to bring a Bible quiz league to my city. My ministry was on top of the Bible quiz world. We won 6 national tournaments and 11 regional championships in the course of our Bible quiz career with the Youth Evangelism Association and with the World Bible Quiz Association. We had a lot to lose, but the truth was worth it, because if we were wrong about the Bible version that we were using, then our ministry was on the wrong side of truth and history. The truth was the only thing that could set us free. Just like the Bible says.

Investigate

Faced with an awful dilemma I began to investigate the issue. If I could have it my way I would have preferred to have discovered that the NIV was just fine. I would arm myself to refute the defenders of the preserved Word of God with all of my information, and defend my little Bible quiz league baby, and be justified in myself, believing that I did not sin against God. I wanted the NIV position to win in my investigation, because I did not want my *comfort zones* challenged. I liked what was going on in my ministry. After all, I was getting hundreds of kids into what I thought was the Bible, so for what should I be ashamed?

A good friend of mine offered me a book that was entitled, *An Understandable History of the Bible* by Dr. Samuel Gipp. This book was later revised and called, *Gipp's Understandable History of the Bible.* Dr. Gipp changed the title in honor of his dad. I confess that my attitude was one of pride, but my friend asked me to promise that if I was to receive the book, that I would read it and not just say that I did. My honor overtook my *pride*, and I was determined to read the book quickly. In my heart of hearts, I believed that I could render a defense of my use of the NIV against these *"King James Only People"* that I had heard about.

It was somewhere around chapter three, as I recall, that Dr. Gipp mentioned the Roman Catholic Jesuits, and their involvement in the changing of the Protestant and Baptist Bible. Remember, Baptists are not Protestants. The same Holy Spirit that delivered me from Catholic indoctrination and led me to the Gospel, was now alerting me to change my attitude and investigate with a heart that wanted to know the truth, and a heart that wanted to obey that truth. This was right in the Lord for me to do. God got my attention, and I read through the book. *I could not believe how wrong I was all those years.* God showed me in the spiritual way that I prayed for, that I had my kids on the *wrong side of truth and history.* We were Bible quizzing in a counterfeit Bible.

The comparative verses used in the book were overwhelming evidence for me to investigate further. I now believed that this was a problem that should not be ignored, or swept under the rug. Little did I know what spiritual battle lay ahead for me. The devil was ripping mad. Believe me, I felt his vengeance against my quest for the truth, almost immediately. An intense investigative study was to follow.

Another friend who was aware of my dilemma, who believed that the NIV and all the modern Bible versions were just fine, bought me a book called, *The*

King James Only Controversy by James White. The devil was making a desperate attempt to confuse me concerning the truth that I was praying to believe. This book is falsely lauded by many scholars who gave it great reviews. This spiritual battle was on.

White's book vexed my spirit. White never answered the questions I was asking. I found the answers to my questions in Dr. Gipp's two books. (See suggested reading section.) Thank God that I read Dr. Gipp's "works" first. The more I read White's book, the more I could see, that the devil was doing everything in his power, to keep me in the NIV. But this only enabled me to have more resolve for the truth, and I began to read every book that I could find, concerning this subject. God strengthened my resolve, and answered my prayer for the truth. Not only did he help me to see this truth *spiritually*, but he gave me the *historical* and *intellectual* knowledge to stand on that truth as well. I began to ask more questions.

Ask Questions

I developed an understanding of both sides of the story. I was now in position to know the truth as God was at work revealing it to me. I still had questions to sort out all this information and to be sure that I got it right because if I was wrong (and I was), then there was going to be all kinds of drastic changes that must go on in my ministry. I better get this right. I turned to a lot of people that I thought were my friends. When push came to shove most of them abandoned my ministry. I remembered that Dr. Gipp had predicted that a stand for the preserved Word of God in English would likely produce this kind of reaction.

As I mentioned in my testimony, I lost friends, board members, and much of my missionary support. None of these people could answer my questions. None of these people did a comparative study, as I implored for them to do. If they would only investigate on their own, perhaps I could educate through this dilemma, and take my ministry back to the preserved Word of God, with everybody staying with me. Only one board member made any kind of attempt to do some studying. This same board member saw some truth in what I was trying to say, but ultimately followed the many modern Bible proponents that were in his life, especially his wife.

This board member also left my ministry. The devil was trying to drive my wife and I out of the ministry altogether. I attempted to slowly convince the

World Bible Quiz Association, to make a move to Bible Quiz in the King James, on the national level. I already started a local King James Bible quiz division. I was on the board of the World Bible Quiz Association, so I managed to get a King James Division started on the national level, along with another board member whom I was able to convince to join me.

We had to rewrite all of the questions. This did not last but only for a few years, because we never did receive the support that we needed to sustain the few troops that we had. One church in our local area pulled their teams out of my local King James League, because my radio program at the time was speaking out publicly against the NIV. Another church in my program left our league because of a miscommunication between the pastor and the youth leader, who I fully informed, that the organization we belonged to nationally, also used the NIV. When his pastor found out, he pulled his teams from our city-wide league. I thought he knew. He did not believe us when we told him we were in the process of converting all the NIV quizzers, but that we needed time. He decided he should not make a difference. He piously pulled his teams out of our local league.

Another church left our ministry to start another league. They lasted one year on their own, and quit quizzing. No one really had any answers to my many questions, during all of this time. I was finding answers in the Bible and in the books that God had brought my way.

I encourage you to ask some of the questions that I began to ask. Do not rest until you get a satisfactory answer. Here is just a sample of the questions that I was asking. You can buy the *Answer Book* by Dr. Sam Gipp that is listed in the suggested reading section. I will list just 12 of 62 questions that are covered in this book. These are some questions that I had, and that you may also have. Here they are:

1. Aren't there archaic words in the Bible, and don't we need a modern translation to eliminate them?

2. Don't the best manuscripts support the new versions?

3. Where do Bible manuscripts come from?

4. Where was the Bible before the 1611 King James Version?

5. Isn't the devil behind all the confusion and fighting over Bible versions?

6. Who were Westcott & Hort?

7. Is the New International Version trustworthy?

8. Should we make an issue of Bible translations?

9. Hasn't the King James Bible been revised?

10. Aren't King James Bible believers a cult?

11. Do the King James Bible believers worship the Bible?

12. What about my friends and future if I stand for the King James Bible?[20]

These are just a few of the many questions that I asked. Not one pastor who used a modern Bible had an answer for me. Neither did the people who abandoned my ministry. There was only one pastor who gave me the time of day, whose kids quizzed in our league, that did any investigation on his own. This pastor saw the truth and obeyed it. Together we presented the evidence to his whole congregation. The church unanimously switched to the King James Bible. There was no division. All the people could see that the pastor's teaching concerning the preserved Word of God was true. After you ask all the questions, and you get the right answers, start to *study yourself approved of God,* so you can defend your position, and the devil will not get the victory. You must *"rightly divide the word of truth."*

Study

Make sure you have some important verses committed to *memory.* You must be able to turn to some comparative verses *on the spot.* You may not have a list handy. Most conversations about this issue are not at a study table where the Bible is actually being opened and compared. It is usually a verbal conversation where the eyes are not looking directly into the Bible. It is easy for some pastor or church leader to refute you verbally, with some comment about those *"King James Only People."* But if you put a few verses into their hands in writing, for them to compare, they will sense that you did your homework, and that you know what you are talking about. Start off with the statement that Jesus, our Saviour, *"falls"* in the modern Bible versions.

Memorize the verses that prove this and then go on to state that Jesus also *"sins"* in his own Bible. The more verses that you have off the top of your head, the better your initial verbal conversation will be. Memorize a verse or two like Matthew 18:11 and Matthew 17:21 that are flat out missing in many modern Bibles. Both of these verses have doctrinal significance. Ask them to look these verses up and then watch their reaction when they cannot find these verses in their Bible.

---

20. Gipp. *The Answer Book,* (See Table of Contents.)

Make an appointment with the pastor, or some leader who is on the elder board. I recommend that you do a Bible study with a close friend from the church. Bring your material and don't let them take their eyes away from being in the Bible. Do a comparative study. Have your *Answer Book*, by Dr. Sam Gipp, ready. When the honest questions come against the preserved Word of God, you will be able to give an answer to all of the questions. *Match sword for sword.* You and your study partner will experience the Bible speaking for itself. The Holy Spirit will be present in all the hearts that are physically at the study. There is only one verse in the Bible that commands us to study. It is a powerful verse found in II Timothy 2:15:

"Study to shew thyself approved unto God, a workman that needeth not to be ashamed, rightly dividing the word of truth."

This verse is about getting *"God's approval"* in your effort to study His word. It is not about just *"doing your best,"* as the modern Bible versions implore you to do. Our best may not be good enough to *"rightly divide the truth."* The truth is what we are trying to find out. Make sure you know beyond a shadow of a doubt that it was the Holy Spirit who convicted you of the truth. When you know the truth in your own heart, because the Holy Spirit convicted you of this truth, you can enter the study with complete confidence that your defense of the King James Bible is a *correct* stand for God.

This is very important. Do not be intimidated by *conflict* and *division*. The *nature* of truth is divisive. That is why we "rightly divide" it. The enemy is the one who has lied, and who has brought this division in our Bible. Those of us who defend the preserved Word of God, want to *unify* on the only Bible we need. We all need God's choice, and we all need God's way. It is God's way concerning our Salvation, and it is God's way concerning His Word.

Admit That There is a Problem

If a person does not see something to be a problem, *then they cannot fix the problem.* When we see that water is dripping from our ceiling, we are forced to admit that there is a hole in our roof. It would be very frustrating if we proclaimed to someone that water is dripping from the ceiling, only to have them deny that the roof needs to be fixed. The proof is in the pudding. There is either a puddle on the floor, or the floor is dry. The problem is obvious.

Defenders of the modern Bible versions do not want to admit that there is a problem. The problem does not exist in their blinded eyes. They *ignore* and *bypass* the problem. Their actions say that if you ignore the problem, and don't bring the problem up to anybody in a conversation, then the problem would just go away. After 130 years, *the problem is still here.* The roof is not only leaking, it has caved in completely. How long will it take you to *"admit that there is a problem?"*

When we are totally convinced that there is a problem, we are better able to put our mind to focus on fixing whatever the problem has damaged. It is never too late to change. A repentance/revival can be possible when each individual has committed themselves to working on their own spiritual walk.

Revival begins with each one of us on a personal level. After all, we claim to have a *personal relationship with Jesus Christ.* We all have to say that each one of us is the *beginning point,* that will open up the possibility of God visiting us with a real repentance/revival in our time. How much do we want to *focus on this?*

First, Go to Your Pastor Alone

The time has come. You have done your homework. You are absolutely convinced that we have a Bible available to us in English and that it is the King James Bible. There are many scholars, leaders and pastors who love to hate this Bible. You know that you are in an important spiritual battle, but you must contend for the truth anyway, and hope that these men see the error of their ways, and are open to be taught. You are hoping that the problem was one of *ignorance* and not one of *indifference.* It is time to make an appointment with your pastor.

I have already mentioned the spiritual battle that is going on in this issue. Prayer is going to be vital. Pray to the Lord that He gives you wisdom concerning the words that you will speak. Pray that your pastor will listen. Pray that when you meet there will be no distractions. Pray that the Holy Spirit will truly be at work, and that it is the Lord that is going to do any changing in your pastor.

Call your pastor up on the phone, and tell him that you would like to schedule an hour of his time, so that you can talk to him about some Bible questions that you have. Do not tell him over the phone that you want to discuss the issue of what Bible version he is using. You will risk just having a phone conversation. The Bible would not be open, and it would be easy for him to divert or change your focus. This meeting must occur *face to face* and in accordance with the Matthew 18 principle of going to your brother alone, if you have a conflict with your brother.

Schedule the meeting at your pastor's earliest convenience. Bring a copy of the preserved Word of God with you, and it will not hurt to bring an NIV with you also, or whatever else your pastor happens to use, so your pastor can see it's not just the NIV that is counterfeit.

You should have some comparative verses written down so that you can remember the references. If you can memorize those verses, it will show your pastor that you have done some homework. Take it one verse at a time. Use some verse that has doctrinal significance. Ask your pastor to tell you what his position is on these doctrines. For example, if you agree on the doctrine of the "virgin birth," ask him why the Bible that he is using does not agree with him. Show him Luke 2:33 and let his eyes see this in the Bible from where he preaches.

Take mental note of his explanation. Does he act surprised and concerned? Does he render some excuse that does not support a true answer? This might be a good time to quote from one of the books that you have been reading. If you hit a dead end, then go to the next problem. You have 64,000 different words from which to choose, and over 5,778 verses to explore. You can show him all day, until he sees that you have some valid points, and that your concerns are real. If your efforts fall on deaf ears, and you feel that you did not make progress, then schedule a second appointment and go to step two in the Matthew 18 principle.

Bring a Witness

The Bible tells us in Matthew chapter 18 to take a witness with you, if a problem is not solved between you and your brother on a one on one basis. When you bring another person into the conversation, you make it harder for any pastor, or anyone, to make an excuse for using a counterfeit Bible. By bringing a witness, you make it harder for the pastor to explain why he should be able to do something wrong, like preach from a counterfeit Bible, and still believe he is doing something right.

You are getting the support that you need to make your case, and convince your pastor that it is right for him to change his view, for the sake of the truth.

It is much harder for the pastor to walk away from *two* of you, then to just walk away from *one*. You are causing the pastor to rethink his position. You have put yourself in a position to offer your help. You should not be looking to condemn.

The idea is to fix the problem and teach through the situation. You are not trying to cast blame or point the finger in the direction of any one individual. You are simply trying to work with the best qualified person in the church who can handle this problem in the right manner. *That person is your pastor.* You did it God's way for the sake of God's truth. Hopefully, you will not have to take this problem to the next level. But if you do have to go to step three, the Bible tells us in Matthew 18 what you should do next.

Take the Problem to the Church

You obeyed God, and you followed the procedure for dealing with a problem in the church, as the Matthew 18 principle commands you to do. You did not receive a positive response from your pastor. His answers back to you were only a justification and a rationalization of the position that he has taken. You know the wrong spirit is present, and even the witness that you brought with you, was to no effect. Your pastor has decided to preach in a counterfeit Bible with or without your approval. What should you do next?

You should notify your pastor that you have no recourse but to take this issue to the church. *Do not do this behind his back.* Let him know that you are willing to continue to help him through this problem, and that he himself can bring the issue before the congregation, if he needs more time to investigate. But notify him that your next move is to ask for permission to address the elders of the church at the next elder meeting. Make sure your pastor is present at the meeting.

Proceed without interruption to take your case before the leaders in the church, who make all the decisions. Hand out in writing the points you wish to make, and be willing to listen to the objections that might come against you. Prepare to have an answer ready for those objections. You should have studied this issue for yourself. You should have read many good books, and you should have the conviction of the Holy Spirit in your heart. Do not be *intimidated* by the fact that everyone in the room might disagree with you.

You are encouraging the elders of the church, in the presence of your pastor, *to think about what they have done.* You never know, there may be someone in the room who says that this issue needs further investigation. You never know, how the Holy Spirit may be working in the hearts of those who are present. You are doing what you know you should do, and in the way that you should do it. You cannot control the reaction that you are going to get. *But you can make a stand for the truth.*

You have earned the right to go before the church as a member in good standing. You pay your tithes and offerings, and you participate in the worship service of the church. You may even be a worker in the church on several committees, or someone who helps with the youth group. Treat everyone with respect, and make sure that you do not show any *anger*. You are not trying to show everyone that you are angry. You are trying to bring a great change in the church that you love. *You are taking on this task for the sake of the truth.*

If your church gets this problem corrected, they can solve any problem in the church, because they will have the right Bible in their hand, and they will have learned the right procedure. They will use this Bible with the conviction of the Holy Spirit, who will guide them to interpret the Bible with proper doctrine. Who knows where God can guide the church concerning all truth. A great step for revival in the church can be gained. *You are giving God a chance to honor your effort.*

God will do His part, but will the leaders of your church have the right attitude toward God? It will be interesting to see how they will handle your concern. You will see just what kind of people you have aligned yourself to fellowship with in the church. Are they showing any concern for the truth? Do they show a reasonable amount of respect for your concern? What should you do next if your efforts have fallen on deaf ears and on blind eyes?

Make it Public

Do not leave the room angry, but let the leaders know that you are disappointed with their response, and that you are going to speak to the other members of the congregation. Be right up front about this, so that it is not perceived against you that *you are the problem.* The rest of the congregation has a right to know that the leadership of the church has led them into a counterfeit Bible. The issue does matter, and the issue is vitally important to the repentance/revival that everyone seems to be talking about. You will find out real quick just what kind of church you belong to when it comes to the truth.

Suggest to the members of the church, that are giving you a listening ear, that they can ask leadership to bring someone to the congregation to *debate the issue openly.* All of the members of the church should be aware of this problem. The members of the church should also make an appointment with the pastor to express their concern. Maybe the issue will be addressed in Sunday school? But make sure that both sides are represented in the classes. Perhaps you can volunteer to teach a class on this yourself?

It might be a good idea to put some good study material into the hands of the congregation. When they see with their eyes the comparative verses, and how they have been changed, they are going to ask a lot of questions. I would encourage them to bring a King James Bible to the service and make some notes on what is different when the pastor preaches from his counterfeit. Make it a point to show him what the real Bible says. Remind him again that you are still gravely concerned, over the use of counterfeit Bibles in your church. Remind him again that you are saddened that you did not get the right response to your concern.

Tell him that you are praying for him to see this truth for himself. Offer to have some personal study time with your pastor, and invite some of the other members of the church to study with you, if they are also concerned about this situation. Don't let the problem go away. Do not add to the problem, by threatening to leave the church just yet. But before you get to the point where you must leave the church, *seek to make a difference.* Make a real honest effort to change the things that you can. Seek to win over several members of the congregation, and let leadership know that you do mean business, and that you honestly want a solution that will not compromise your convictions.

Make a Difference

Do you see the need for change? Can you see why it is impossible for God to visit us in this age of Laodicea as things are right now? I have suggested that you not leave your church *just yet.* You have to make an honest effort to be a difference maker. It has been said that if you are not part of the *solution*, then you are part of the *problem.* Continue to communicate with your pastor and with the elders of the church, but let them know that you are still concerned. Be open and up front about your conviction and prove to your pastor that you are a *friend* and not his *enemy.* Show them you just want to *stand for the truth* and that you believe they do too. Give the situation a reasonable amount of time to come to a happy conclusion. You will know when it is time that you simply have to *leave the church,* but not until you gave it your best effort to make a difference.

Continue with your focus, and make sure that the issue does not go away. Pastors like to "ignore" and "bypass" this issue. They know that when push comes to shove, and the issue is out in the open, they do not have a leg to stand on. The corruption will be too obvious to the people. In order for you to make a difference, you must *persevere* until there is change. God will honor your obedience, and He will give you the strength that you need to stay on the course.

Write a Letter

Write an open letter to the whole church and explain to them why you have taken a stand against the counterfeit Bible that is being used in your church. Challenge each and every member, and those who are in leadership, along with the pastor, to *investigate* what you have *discovered* to be *true.* Make sure you write down several of the verses that you learned in your comparative study, and show the comparison verses in your letter, so everyone can see it in black and white. Writing a letter is a very *effective* way to *communicate.* You are making a difference by putting the issue to the forefront. Writing a letter is *powerful.*

You are challenging everybody to do their own investigation, just like you did. You are opening up the door for the Holy Spirit to really move in your church. *It might not be comfortable at first.* False comfort and false peace is *not* the objective. *Truth,* and *revival,* and *obedience to God,* and putting God in the *position to bless you* and your *church,* should be the reason for your concern.

Offer the opportunity to *debate the issue publicly.* Let everyone see who the people are who want to keep things just as they are without any goals for improvement. More and more members of the church may start to bring their King James Bible to the service. Several of the members can now correct the pastor when he preaches from a counterfeit, and when it is obvious that your Bible had said something different.

Hand Out Some Tracts

Another effective way to communicate with people, is to *hand them a tract.* Tracts get right to the point on a certain issues, like a doctrine of the Bible. They are short and to the point, and powerful, when you want to communicate the things that are true in your Bible. Tracts encourage other people to *stop and think.* Tracts have a way of detailing the facts right in plain view. There are many tracts available on the subject of counterfeit Bibles. In the suggested reading section of this book, you can find out where you can purchase some of the greatest tracts that are written on this subject.

Make sure your pastor gets a copy of the tracts that you are handing out. You are doing all of this right up front and not behind his back. You never have to *ever* be ashamed of the truth. The truth will set you free, just like the Bible says it will do. There is no need for any apologies to be given. You did not do anything wrong. You defended the truth, and proved your position. You made a stand for God.

I have handed out hundreds of tracts to many people. You can get all the tracts you need at Daystar Publishing. (See the suggested reading section.) The response has been positive over 95% of the time. It is interesting how someone who is not in leadership position can easily discern these counterfeit Bibles. The problem is not so much with the people, as it is with leadership. Leadership would rather be blind then to invade their comfort zones. Leadership does not want to admit that they are wrong for using a counterfeit Bible.

Meet With Those Who Agree With You

You are going to be surprised at how many people, who were left in the dark on this issue, will now come *out of the woodwork.* Just about every individual that I have shared this subject with on a personal level, has given me a positive response. So many of these people ask me for more tracts, and are so appreciative to me that I have alerted them to look into this problem. Some of these people are now teaching other people these same truths. The true church is an *organism.* It is made up of people who are saved, and who are following the Holy Spirit. People who love their Bible, and who study their Bible, will see these truths very clearly. The Holy Spirit promises to guide all of us into the truth of God.

Find out who the people are who agree with you on what you have presented. Meet with them and make sure everybody knows that the meeting is not a secret. Come up with a game plan to keep the issue to the forefront. You do not need to surrender to the devil. If you have to leave the church, then take a few people with you. You have now put your pastor and the elders of the church in the position to consult with the denominational leaders. Hopefully, we will bring our colleges back to where they need to be.

Hopefully, these leaders will report to the scholars, and the professors of their colleges, that the people are very concerned about the Bibles that they are producing. Leadership will be held accountable, or it will be forced to be replaced. Put the leaders at risk. Let them see that they may lose you, and several other members of the church. Or, the church itself may leave the denomination altogether. (Another reason not to leave your church too hastily – your pastor could have the courage to make this move; another reason prayer is needed. We are commanded to pray for our pastors.)

There is probably a church somewhere in your neighborhood who preaches from the preserved Word of God. Of course, you must test their other doctrines, as well. You never know how God will bless the obedience that you and some other people of your church have displayed.

If you and several other people have to leave your church, remember that you were not the problem. You responded to a problem that these leaders created for you. If you have to leave, it was because they forced your hand, by refusing to change their counterfeit Bible. It was their choice to remain disobedient to God. You, and the other members of your church did everything that you could do to bring the right solution to the problem. There are two more things that you should do.

Throw Away the Counterfeit Bibles

Do not use the counterfeit Bibles for your personal devotions. It is time to buy a King James Bible, if you haven't already done so. It is alright to keep a copy of one of the modern version Bibles, but only as a reference point in your comparative study efforts. Stop buying from the publishers and bookstores that produce all kinds of products that water down, who you are to be in Christ. Study guides are available in the King James Version. You do not need the counterfeit material to help you understand something better. The King James Bible is a modern English Bible. It has an older dialect, but it is only a 5th grade reading level.

The King James Bible is written in the purest of English. More importantly, you are no longer participating in the game plan of the devil, who wants to destroy the preserved Word of God. Although it is impossible for the devil to destroy the preserved Word of God, he can render it useless by putting you and your fellow church members on something else that God forbids. Don't let the devil lead your pastor into telling you that this is alright. Follow the Holy Spirit.

Your purchase of these counterfeit Bibles, keep enabling the devil to build on the momentum that he has gained, since the early 1970's. The Word of God has been peddled to the people for profit. You bought the Bibles, and the commentaries, and you are the one who is keeping them in business. You will be just as guilty as they are when judgment comes your way, if you continue to use these counterfeits. Now that you know that this is a blatant *disobedience* against God, don't hurt your relationship with Jesus. You *obey*, whether the people around you obey or not. If push comes to shove, then LEAVE YOUR CHURCH.

Leave Your Church

My heart breaks at the thought of making this suggestion to you. So many people leave their church for all of the *wrong reasons*. Many people, who have caused division in their church over some of the most stupid reasons, have never returned to a body of believers. Many pastors have had to unjustly bear the scars of people getting mad at them for no reason at all. This is a poor witness unto Christ, and it does not further the cause of the church in any way. The Bible tells us in Hebrews 10:25:

"Not forsaking the assembling of ourselves together, as the manner of some is; but exhorting one another, and so much the more, as ye see the day approaching."

Going to church is very important. The church is the established institution of God. The church has been ordained by God Himself. No man can grow in his relationship with Christ without the help of some other believers that are to be involved in his/her life. There are many reasons for believers to congregate together at a certain time and place. The church has been established by God for our edification. The problem we are facing is *"what on earth is the true church?"* Is it possible that the church you are attending is not a true New Testament Church?

If any local church does not preach from the preserved Word of God, and it does not stand for the doctrines of belief that are outlined in the Bible, it has forfeited its own standing as a church that is walking with God. It is true that there is no perfect church to be found anywhere. If you find one, then stay away from that church, because your presence will make it imperfect. But there are certain lines to be drawn from Scripture that make a church a true church of God. Following and obeying the Scripture, and having the right Scriptures before you, are certainly in line with what a true New Testament Church would teach.

The final authority for any *true* New Testament Church is the Bible. If the Bible is not *inerrant, inspired, infallible,* and *perfectly preserved*, then it cannot be of God. There are counterfeit Bibles, and there are counterfeit churches. You do not have to align yourself with a counterfeit church. It is one thing for the true church to be made up of imperfect people who are striving, then for a counterfeit church to possess, and to use a counterfeit Bible.

Imperfect people can *change* and *improve*, and move *forward*. But a church that follows a counterfeit Bible can never please God. If the devil succeeds in destroying the foundation that makes a true church a true church of God, he in essence could damage that church. It is impossible according to the Scriptures, for the devil to destroy the true church of God. But he sure can damage the churches that operate outside of Scripture.

The preserved Word of God will keep the devil from having any final victory over the church of God. But the devil sure does want to do as much damage as our leadership will let him do. Many of our pastors are leading the way. Only you can help them face their "alma maters." Many pastors worship their "alma maters." Our pastors have to admit that they were trained by scholars and professors, who chose to follow the devil when it came to the final authority of the Scriptures. They played right into the hands of the Roman Catholic Jesuits.

You do not have to participate in the devil's game plan. After you have exhausted all of your options, helping your church come back to the preserved Word of God in English, and after all of your efforts have failed, YOU MUST LEAVE YOUR CHURCH, and find one that preaches the *truth*. This is the right thing for you to do, unless you become part of the problem. You will be guilty by association. The Bible instructs us on how to deal with people who refuse to walk in the truth, once God has shown them something to be true. Once again take heed of the verse found in I Timothy 6:4-5:

"He is proud, knowing nothing, but doting about questions and strifes of words, whereof cometh envy, strife, railings, evil surmisings, perverse disputings of men of corrupt minds, and destitute of the truth, supposing that gain is godliness: from such withdraw thyself."

Do not feel guilty. You have done everything the way the Bible instructed you to do. You followed the procedure given to you by Jesus in Matthew chapter 18. You even stayed on a little longer than maybe you had to, but you know that you gave it an honest shot for the sake of truth. You are free. You can LEAVE. There is a church close to you that will preach from the preserved Word of God in English. The preserved Word of God in English has proven itself over time. If the preserved Word of God cannot be found as the King James Bible, then it cannot be found anywhere. The Bible that came from God is not *lost*, it is not being *used*. I cannot point my finger at God for letting His Word disappear from the earth, can you? Which Bible is in your hand?

A Letter to My Catholic Family and Friends

Colossians 2:8 says this:

"Beware lest any man spoil you through philosophy and vain deceit, after the tradition of men, after the rudiments of the world, and not after Christ."

If any *"tradition"* of man is not in the Bible, it cannot be a *"final authority"* when it comes to the *"truth."* There is a *true "church tradition"* that lines up with the Bible. The Roman Catholic Church has its own *"man-made tradition."* The Roman Catholic Church puts its *"man-made tradition"* on a pedestal equal with *"Scripture."* Actually when push comes to shove the Catholic Church puts *"tradition"* ahead of *"Scripture."* Roman Catholic Church tradition *usurps* the Scripture whenever it is convenient for them to create their own *unbiblical* doctrines. *That cannot be done!* To do so is *heresy.*

Whenever the Catholic Church feels attacked by someone who exposes their *"unbiblical, doctrinal beliefs"* they label the person as a *"catholic basher."* The term implies that the Catholic Church has been *"wronged"* and is *"unfairly"* being attacked. If someone reads something that is *negative* toward the Catholic Church, and brings what is being written or said to the Catholic authorities, then the church officials justify themselves by telling their people not to read or to listen to such nonsense by the *"catholic basher."* The *"catholic basher"* is someone who *"hates"* in their eyes. But don't you have a right to investigate the truth for yourself? You sure do!

My friends, there is a big difference in *"catholic bashing"* and what is really just a telling of the *"truth."* If I as a Christian, and you as a Catholic, am a *"defender of truth,"* then let us both *study* ourselves approved of God, and let God be *true* and all *men* to be *liars* like the Bible says. Let our positions be backed by the *"word of God"* and not by our *"man made doctrines and traditions."* The Bible and church history have exposed what the Catholic Church really believes. Certain things are simply facts that no *"counter labeling"* can change. If I am a *"hater"* then I must hate my own family. Both my family and I know that is not true.

There is a difference between the *"catholic laity"* (the Bible says *"flock"*) and the *"Roman Catholic hierarchy."* There are many wonderful Roman Catholic people who simply choose to be deceived by their hierarchy. I do not doubt that they are *"good people."* Some may have a sincere relationship with Jesus. Those who get saved tend to leave the church after they study their Bible. My family fits into that category. They are good people by the world's standards. My family and I are very close, despite our biblical differences. So, for anyone to accuse me of being a *"catholic hater"* will have to accuse me of hating my own family. Again, *it simply is not true.* My family knows this.

What I do hate is the fact that the hierarchy lies against the Bible to my family and friends, and ultimately deceives them on *"how to be saved."* I prayed 38 years for God to *"assure"* me of my parent's Salvation before they died. My mom just recently passed away. I finally was assured that she was saved as she had confessed with her mouth the Lord Jesus. I was there when she professed, so I heard it. When my dad died at age 94, seven months before my mom had passed away, I did not have that assurance until at his bedside, and before his last breath, God answered my 38 year prayer, and assured me that my dad was ready for eternity. If you ever want to know what happened in this story, I will tell it to you. My younger brother Dominick was a witness.

I also have several friends who are Roman Catholic. Most of my Catholic family and friends are *"Bible illiterate."* I do not say that to *hurt, judge,* or *condemn.* They are simply a product of what their hierarchy has always *decided* for them. The Roman Catholic hierarchy does not want them to *know the Scriptures, or church history,* unless it is in a controlled situation. *Yes,* this is *their* policy. They claim that only the church is qualified to *"interpret the Scriptures."*

The Catholic Church believes that its hierarchy is more qualified than the Holy Spirit himself. The church does not trust in the Holy Spirit working in a *saved* person, guiding that person into a proper interpretation of biblical truth. It claims that the people cannot understand the Bible. In reality, the Catholic Church *fears* the Bible being in the hands of the people, because the church knows that it cannot stop the Holy Spirit, who guides the believer into all truth, and when a believer reads a 5th grade reading level Bible, the Catholic Church knows that they will easily discern the false doctrines that the Roman Catholic Church invented. Also, the church never taught them the two rules of *"interpreting the Scriptures,"* in the first place. Those two rules are as follows:

1. Wherever the English appears vague:

Go to God and ask Him for wisdom, and understanding. Check the Greek wherever it is accurate.

2. Wherever there is a doubt concerning a *doctrine.* Then we should: *"check Scripture with Scripture."*

When I was indoctrinated into the Roman Catholic system from birth, I was never encouraged to participate in a home Bible study, or to have a time of personal devotions. In John 17:17 the Bible says:

"Sanctify them through thy truth: thy word is truth."

All truth must line up with Scripture. The Bible commands us to *study* these Scriptures in II Timothy 2:15 and in I Thessalonians 4:10-11. If you find yourself asking a question, the Holy Spirit working through God's Word, and godly people, will always find you an answer. The truth will be confirmed by that same Holy Spirit, and not by some *man, church or movement.* You will confirm the right answer by God living in you. He cannot be wrong. You will *discern* the difference.

The greatest enemy of the Roman Catholic Church is not the individual *"catholic basher."* The greatest enemy of the Roman Catholic Church is the *"Bible itself."* The Roman Catholic Church has an *argument* with God that the church chooses not to *settle.* The Catholic Church refuses to adhere to the Bible. The church itself created its own doctrines and beliefs outside of Scripture. The church has many *"apologists"* who are paid *"good money."* They certainly have a lot for which to *"apologize."*

The Catholic Church eliminates the Holy Spirit as being qualified to be the *"true vicar of Christ."* The church makes you feel *"stupid"* and *"unqualified"* to interpret the Scriptures even though the Holy Spirit lives in you when you get saved. The church intentionally keeps their people *"ignorant."*

If you are a Catholic reading this book, and if you have a beef as to what is being written about your church, your beef is with your Roman Catholic authorities who have lied to you from the beginning, and not with me. Search the Scriptures, and church history, and study for yourself, whether your doctrines are true. Here are some questions that you should ask. I am going to give you just one Scripture per question to look up so that you can examine this for yourself. There are several Scriptures that could be listed, but for the sake of time I will only list one per question, unless otherwise stated.

Who is the *"vicar of Christ"* the *"pope"* or the *"Holy Spirit?"* Luke 24:49. This is a verse on the *"ascension of Jesus."* Jesus gives some final instructions before He ascends.

Are priests a part of the fivefold Gospel laid out in Ephesians chapter 4? (Ephesians 4:11)

Do we confess our *sins* to a priest or do we confess our *faults* one to another? James 5:16

Has the Bible authorized the *"sacrifice of a mass?"* Read all of Hebrews 8-10.

Is Salvation *"instantaneous"* or *"progressive?"* I Corinthians 1:18. (Don't forget to use the preserved Word of God concerning this verse because the Roman Catholic inspired counterfeits have changed this verse, in the modern corrupted versions.)

Are we saved by "works and faith?" Ephesians 2:8-9.

Is it possible that the system of *"works and faith"* can actually be grouped together for Salvation? Romans 11:6.

Is Mary *"sinless?"* Leviticus chapter 12; Luke 1:46-47; Luke 2:22; (I listed 3 here because this can be sensitive.)

Is Mary a *"perpetual virgin?"* Matthew 1:25. (The counterfeits also changed this Roman Catholic inspired verse as well.)

Should we pray the *"rosary?"* Matthew 6:7.

Can *"Mary"* and the *"saints"* be mediators between us and God? I Timothy 2:5.

Is there a place called *"purgatory"* in the Bible? Hebrews 9:27 and Luke 23:43 when Jesus told the thief on the cross this statement:

"Verily I say unto thee, today shalt thou be with me in paradise."

Should we call a *"priest"* father? Matthew 23:9.

Is the *"pope"* infallible even when he speaks *"ex cathedra?"* Romans 3:23.

Can a Catholic or any person *"know"* that they are saved? I John 5:10 and I John 5:13. (I listed two verses here because it is a *"sin of presumption"* for a Catholic to believe that they are saved while on the earth.)

Many books have been written on the false doctrines of the Roman Catholic Church. The Roman Catholic Church preaches *"another gospel."* It has a system of Salvation by *"works and sacraments."* Catholics believe that they have an *"apostolic connection to the early church."* Church history shows that they did not even come on the scene until after the *"donation of Constantine."* This happened in 325 A.D.

In concluding this letter, I want you to know that no one should ever have to make an apology for the truth just because someone else feels hurt. If you do not like what has been written about the Catholic Church, you should challenge your priest to explain to you why the Catholic Church puts *church tradition"* ahead of the *"Bible"* when it comes to *"final authority."* Research the many forgeries that were written by the Catholic Church concerning their false history, and their false connection to the early church. In particular you can look up the *"Pseudo-Isidorian Decretals."*

The Pseudo-Isidorian Decretals are proven forgeries of supposed letters from the supposed early church popes, who succeeded the first, so-called pope, Peter. The Scripture in Matthew 16, that the Roman Catholic Church uses to proclaim Peter as pope, is *misinterpreted*. The same church accuses the Bible believer of that same misinterpretation. It is called "double speak." A study of the English text, and the preserved Greek, and checking *"Scripture with Scripture,"* will *clearly* reveal the *correct* interpretation.

I have a Catholic inspired Greek New Testament in my office and I looked up the Greek rendering concerning Petros and Petra. I wanted to see if the Catholic inspired Greek New Testament of Westcott and Hort dared to change Petros/Petra to Petros/Petros. Even the Catholic inspired Greek text of Westcott and Hort had Petros/Petra.

The Greek student knows that Jesus was talking to Peter about Himself. This is indicated by the rendering of Petros to Petra in the Greek. The church was to be built on Jesus, the *Rock*, and not Peter the *stone*. You would think that the Catholic inspired Greek would have caught this and changed the Greek to Petros/Petros. But I guess they know that their people are not going to go to the Greek when it comes to a doctrine, so they either forgot this or they left it alone. Maybe they should not have endorsed Westcott and Hort's Greek text in the first place!

There are some 34 additional Scriptures in the Bible that refer to the *Rock*. Every single one of them points to God or Jesus as the *Rock*. Find a concordance and check Scripture with Scripture to properly interpret the Scriptures when it comes to *doctrine*.

Popery has always been cruel to the people. The Catholic Church has killed between 60-80 *million* people in the course of *church history*. Pope John Paul the VI finally apologized for this, but it was a little apology, *a little too late*. The Catholic people never really understood the real ramifications of such an apology.

Sal Varsalone,
The Youthquake Ministry

Beware!

Coming to a bookstore near you! The new and improved Bible of the century. Easier to read, easier to understand. This Bible will usher in the new world government and the new world church. It will unite all mankind to a false truth.

Welcome,
to the
Chrislam Bible.

It is now in its developmental stage.

Google 'the creation of the Chrislam Bible' for more information.

Suggested Reading

1. *Gipp's Understandable History of the Bible* by Dr. Samuel C. Gipp, Th.D. Daystar Publishing, P.O. Box 464, Miamitown Ohio, 45041. 1-800-311-1823. A must read. This book changed the course of my ministry.

2. *The Answer Book* by Dr. Samuel C. Gipp, Th.D. Daystar Publishing, P.O. Box 464, Miamitown Ohio, 45041. 1-800-311-1823 Every attack against the preserved Word of God in English is addressed with a Biblical answer. This book has not been refuted.

3. *Is Our English Bible Inspired?* by Dr. Samuel C. Gipp, Th.D. Daystar Publishing, P.O. Box 464, Miamitown Ohio, 45041. 1-800-311-1823. Is our King James Bible perfect or just a good translation?

4. *A Chartered History of the Bible* by James C. Kahler, Daystar Publishing, P.O. Box 464, Miamitown Ohio, 45041. 1-800-311-1823. This book is an accurate, simple history, that will help you with your perspective concerning the issue of our Bible.

5. *New Age Bible Versions* by G.A. Riplinger, A.V. Publications Corp. P.O. Box 280, Ararat VA. 24053 USA. 1-800-435-4535. Gail Riplinger examines the trends of where society is going in "new age thinking" and how it is connected to counterfeit Bibles. This book is very good.

6. *In Awe of Thy Word* by G.A. Riplinger, A.V. Publications Corp. P.O. Box 280, Ararat VA. 24053 USA. 1-800-435-4535. Gail Riplinger not only examines words, she examines letters as well. This book is awesome.

7. *If the Foundations Be Destroyed* by Rev. Chick Salliby, Word and Prayer Ministries, P.O. Box 361, Fiskdale, MA. 01518-0361. I do not agree with Chick Salliby's personal position on "tongues," but he writes an excellent book on the preserved Word of God. The tongues issue is not discussed in this book. This book is very easy to read, and it has a great list of Bible verse comparisons.

8. *Purified Seven Times, The Miracle of the English Bible* by Evangelist Bill Bradley, Revival Fires! Publishing, Rd 1, Box 940, Claysburg, PA. 16625. 814-239-2813. Psalm 12:6-7 comes alive as this book shows specific purifications of the Bible in English before the King James is written.

9. *Touch Not the Unclean Thing* By David H. Sorenson, D. Min. Northstar Baptist Ministries, 1820 West Morgan St. Duluth MN. 55811-1878. davidsorenson@juno.com Should a Christian who seeks to live a holy life, include counterfeit Bibles in his walk with God? Is it disobedient to use a counterfeit Bible?

10. *Final Authority, a Christian's Guide to the King James Bible* by William P. Grady, Ph.D. Grady Publications, Inc. P.O. Box 506, 219. The Bible is either our "final authority" or it is not. This book will show us why the Bible is our "final authority" in all matters of faith and practice.

11. *Catamount* by Woody Knowles, G.F. Hutchison Press, 319 South Block Avenue, Suite 17, Fayetteville, AR. 72701. This book is an entertaining fictional story within a story. It will make a great movie someday, if Hollywood finds the courage to make the film.

12. *Manuscript Evidence* by Dr. Peter Ruckman, Pensacola Bible Press, PO Box 86, Paloatka, Florida 32077. Don't let anyone tell you that the KJB scholars added anything to the Scriptures

for which they did not have a manuscript. This book has all the evidence you need and it tells the truth about the Septuagint.

13. *Foxes Book of Martyrs* Fleming H. Revell Company or amazonbooks.com. This book is about the history of the many Christians who died a martyrs' death for Christ at the hands of the Roman Catholic Church and other persecutors of true Christians.

14. *Babylon Mystery Religion, Ancient and Modern* Ralph Woodrow, P.O. Box 124, Riverside, CA 92502-0124. Babylon Mystery Religion is a detailed Biblical and historical account of how, when, why, and where ancient paganism was mixed with Christianity mainly through the Roman Catholic Church.

15. *Catholicism Against Itself* by O.C. Lambert. Bible Publications, Inc, Fort Worth Texas 76118. The Catholic Hierarchy's standard reply to books that attack the Catholic system has always been: "They are written by enemies of the church, and are not true." But "It can't happen here!" Charges in this volume are copied word-for word from official books of the Catholic Church, with titles and page numbers given. So the author, in complete fairness, allows the Catholic Church to speak for herself.

16. *Masonry Beyond the Light* by William Schnoebelen, Chick Publications, P.O. Box 662, Chino CA 91708-0662. 909-987-0771. Fax 909-941-8128. To some, Masonry is just a fine Christian Organization. But to higher level Masons, who know what goes on behind the scenes, it's something much different. Here are the inside secrets of Masonry. If you think a person can be a good Christian and a good Mason, you need the facts that declare that "Lucifer is God." Schnoebelen was a former 32 degree Mason, and a former high Priest in Satanism, before he got saved.

17. You can purchase several great tracts on counterfeit Bibles from Daystar Publishing. Call 1-800-311-1823. These tracts are quick, easy to understand, and right to the point. They are very handy for you to witness to others the truth about counterfeit Bibles.

Bibliography

Bradley, Bill. (1998 or 2001). *Purified Seven Times, The Miracle Of the English Bible*, Claysburg, PA: Revival Fires! Publishing.

Fighting Back! A Handy Reference For King James Bible Believers: Seventy-Five Common Sayings. <http://www.av1611.org/jmelton/fight.html#fight4/>

Gipp, Samuel, Th.D. (Publication Date). *Is Our English Bible Inspired?*, Miamitown, Ohio: Daystar Publishing.

Gipp. (1987). *Gipp's Understandable History of the Bible*, Miamitown, Ohio: Daystar Publishing.

Gipp. (1989 or 2003). *The Answer Book,* Miamitown, Ohio: Daystar Publishing.

Grady, William P., Ph.D. (1993). *Final Authority, A Christian's Guide to the King James Bible.* Schererville, Indiana: Grady Publications, Inc.

The Holy, King James Bible.

The New International Version of the Bible.

Human Computer Chip Studied. <http://www.usatoday.com/news/nation/2002/02/26/chip.htm> (Accessed June 22, 2011).

Kah, Gary P. (1999). *The New World Religion.* Carol Stream, IL: Hope International Publishing.

Kahler, James. (Publication Date). *A Charted History of the Bible*, Miamitown, Ohio: Daystar Publishing.

Ramstack, Tom. (Apr. 15, 2002.) Firm seeks FDA approval for Human microchip implants; the VeriChip is another sign that Sept. 11 has catapulted the effort to secure America into a realm with uncharted possibilities — and possible unintended consequences. Insight on the News(Online magazine). (Referring to the February 26, 2002 article "Human Computer Chip Studied" in <http://www.usatoday.com/news/nation/2002/02/26/chip.htm> (Accessed June 22, 2011), the Feb. 28, 2002 Washington Time article "Firm seeks FDA approval for human chip implants Voluntary use planned for medical data, identification ," etc.)

Riplinger, G. A. (Publication Date). *New Age Bible Versions*, Ararat, VA: A.V. Publications Corp.

Riplinger. (Publication Date). *In Awe of Thy Word,* Ararat, VA: A.V. Publications Corp.

Salliby, Chick. (1994). *If the Foundations Be Destroyed,* Fiskdale, MA: Word and Prayer Ministries.

Sorenson, David H., D.Min. (Publication Date). *Touch Not the Unclean Thing.* Duluth, MN: Northstar Baptist Ministries.

Vance, Lawrence M, Ph.D. (2011). *Archaic Words and the Authorized Version.* Pensacola, FL: Vance Publications.